Guitar Scale Guru

The Scale Book

Your Guide For Success!

By Karl Aranjo

Catalog #07-4088

ISBN# 1-56922-186-3

Printed in the United States of America

Produced by John L. Haag

Cover photo by James Bean, Ojai, CA
Cover photo of Matt Haag

Exclusive Distributor:
CREATIVE CONCEPTS PUBLISHING CORPORATION
6020-B Nicolle Street, Ventura, California 93003
Check out our Web site at *http://www.creativeconcepts.com*
or you can Email us at *mail@creativeconcepts.com*

Melody is Everything

Igor Stravinsky
composer

Melody is what makes music memorable. A beautiful melody, in any style, is the essence of the music. Many of the worlds great guitarists have gained their reputations because of their ability to compose or improvise wonderful, memorable ***melodies.*** Making musical melodies is primarily based on a thorough knowledge of scales and their uses.

Guitar playing requires a complete training and a clear, logical method for the playing and use of scales. The problem is that most scale books are confusing and unfocused. Until now. The book you're holding is packed with clear, practical information and easy to read diagrams. Unlocking the secrets of your guitar will be a pleasure as all of your old questions are answered.

Teachers, students and guitarists of all levels will find this book to be one of the most powerful tools in their entire arsenal. Music is melody and melodies are based on scales. If you want to learn your scales then this is

"The book you've been looking for"

Welcome

You're holding one of the exciting new **reference** books from Creative Concepts publishing: *The Guru Series.* Each book bearing this name is incredibly clear, informative and practical. This material has been carefully tested on hundreds of students and yields fantastic results while appearing to be fun and easy. For today's students and teachers, *The Guru Series* of educational materials represents the best available!!

Special note to teachers....

If you're a professional guitar teacher, you've no doubt been frustrated with traditional guitar books. Most students don't like them and simply won't study them. Aware that the tired old methods of the past don't measure up, students who have these books forced upon them usually quit their guitar lessons.

The newer books are a little better but often contain only a few worthwhile pages and generally don't fit in with your program. You've always felt stifled by them because they won't allow you to teach *your way*.

The Guru Series of *reference books* solve these problems beautifully because they allow you to focus your lessons on the material essential to developing real world playing skills without breaking your rhythm. The *easygrid* © graphics were created especially for this project and are unavailable elsewhere. The diagrams and illustrations in this book are like a breath of fresh air, making teaching and learning a pleasure again.

Special note to students....

If you're serious about learning today's guitar, then you need to have current, top notch material created with someone like you in mind. The book you're holding is *the* serious choice- not just another waste of time and money. Every page of a *Guru Series* book contains only the essential material you want and deserve with none of the bull.

Because this a *reference book* and **is not** part of a "graded" method book series (Book 1, Book 2, etc..) you learn only what **you** want to learn when **you** want to learn it. Each *Guru Series* book is an intensive study providing a wealth of material in specific key areas. *Guru Series* books keep you motivated and enable you to concentrate your efforts where you see fit, keeping **you** in total control of your developing style.

Table of Contents

Table of Contents

About the Author

KARL W. ARANJO is a professional guitarist and guitar instructor based in Southern California. His lifelong guitar studies have included teachers such as Tony Mottolla, Ted Greene & William G. Leavitt, author of the Berklee method.

Karl is a graduate of Boston's Berklee College of Music and the leader of a busy performing band, *Karl Aranjo's Jazz Attack.* When not teaching, learning, performing, writing or recording, Karl enjoys the company of his lovely wife Karen and Roxanne the dog.

Mr. Aranjo welcomes any and all correspondence and inquiries concerning his books and recordings. Please direct your letters to:

CREATIVE CONCEPTS PUBLISHING CORPORATION
6020-B Nicolle Street • Ventura, California 93003
Check out our Web site at *http://www.creativeconcepts.com*
or you can Email us at *mail@creativeconcepts.com*

This book is dedicated to my students...past, present and future -you continue to be a great inspiration, and joy. Special thanks to Graham, Ben, Steven U., Reza, Shirin Z., McArthur, Zak D., Barbe, Marcello S., Al, Pashley, Glickley, Jeff-O, M. Rohn, Amy H., Vern, & Sandeep to name only a few of the students who have meant so much to me . This book is for all of you..... Thanks!

Key- Nomenclature

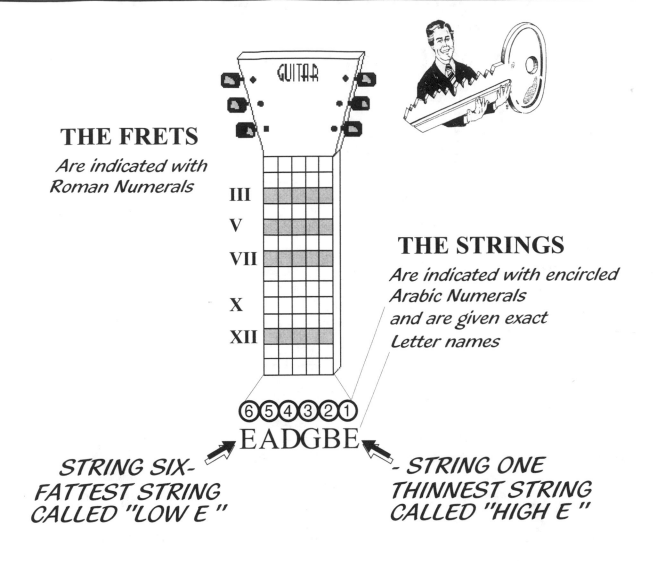

THE FRETS

Are indicated with Roman Numerals

GUITAR

III
V
VII
X
XII

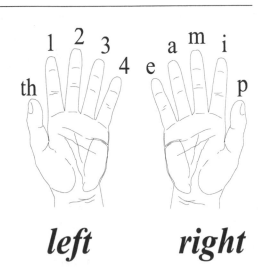

THE STRINGS

Are indicated with encircled Arabic Numerals and are given exact Letter names

⑥⑤④③②①
EADGBE

STRING SIX- FATTEST STRING CALLED "LOW E "

- STRING ONE THINNEST STRING CALLED "HIGH E "

THE FINGERS

Of the **left hand** (fretting hand) are labeled with regular arabic numerals:
 1, 2, 3, 4, & th (for the thumb)

Of the **right hand** (picking hand) are labeled with letters:
P, I, M, A, E.

1 2 3
       4   e a m i
th   p

left   *right*

How to Read Scale Diagrams.

Notes in scales are played in order: first **ascend,** (get higher in pitch) then **descend** (get lower in pitch). In the examples to follow listen for the good old sound of **"Do, Re, Mi, Fa, Sol."**

Example 1

As you slide your finger up the third string, the pitch of the notes becomes higher. Think of this as shortening the string- *using a shorter length of the string to produce a higher pitched note.*

> **The shorter the string, the higher pitched the note.**

Example 2

Correctly playing the notes in example 2 involves switching strings. As you switch strings, think of the thick strings as producing lower notes while the thinner strings produce higher notes.

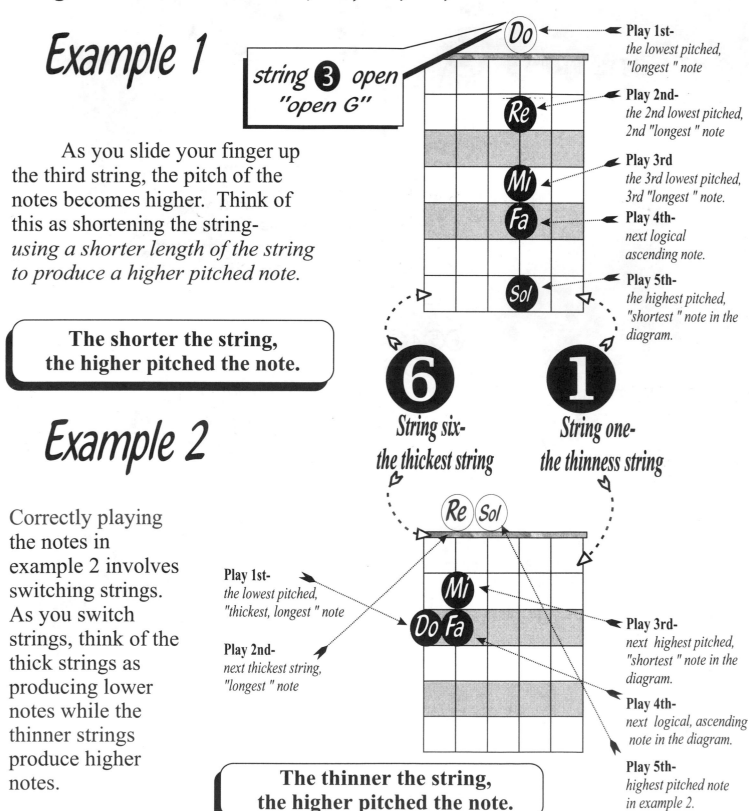

string ❸ *open* "open G"

Play 1st- *the lowest pitched, "longest " note*

Play 2nd- *the 2nd lowest pitched, 2nd "longest " note*

Play 3rd *the 3rd lowest pitched, 3rd "longest " note.*

Play 4th- *next logical ascending note.*

Play 5th- *the highest pitched, "shortest " note in the diagram.*

6 *String six- the thickest string*

1 *String one- the thinness string*

Play 1st- *the lowest pitched, "thickest, longest " note*

Play 2nd- *next thickest string, "longest " note*

Play 3rd- *next highest pitched, "shortest " note in the diagram.*

Play 4th- *next logical, ascending note in the diagram.*

Play 5th- *highest pitched note in example 2.*

> **The thinner the string, the higher pitched the note.**

Scale diagrams are read by playing the lowest pitched note first. Continue from thicker strings to thinner strings, playing all notes on one string before proceeding to the next.

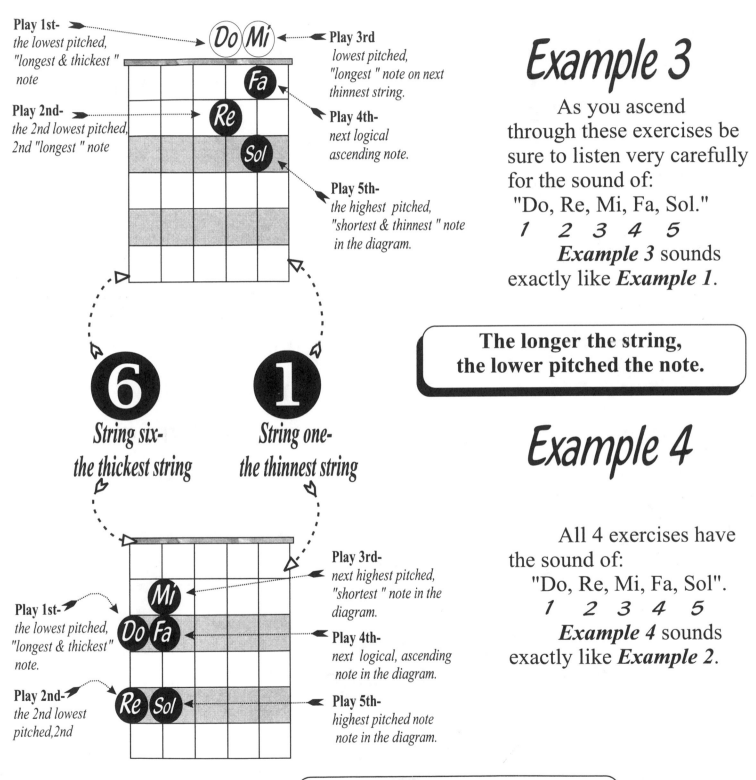

Play 1st-
the lowest pitched, "longest & thickest" note

Play 2nd-
the 2nd lowest pitched, 2nd "longest" note

Play 3rd
lowest pitched, "longest" note on next thinnest string.

Play 4th-
next logical ascending note.

Play 5th-
the highest pitched, "shortest & thinnest" note in the diagram.

6 String six- *the thickest string*

1 String one- *the thinnest string*

Play 1st-
the lowest pitched, "longest & thickest" note.

Play 2nd-
the 2nd lowest pitched, 2nd

Play 3rd-
next highest pitched, "shortest" note in the diagram.

Play 4th-
next logical, ascending note in the diagram.

Play 5th-
highest pitched note note in the diagram.

Example 3

As you ascend through these exercises be sure to listen very carefully for the sound of:
"Do, Re, Mi, Fa, Sol."
1   2   3   4   5
Example 3 sounds exactly like **Example 1**.

The longer the string, the lower pitched the note.

Example 4

All 4 exercises have the sound of:
"Do, Re, Mi, Fa, Sol".
1   2   3   4   5
Example 4 sounds exactly like **Example 2**.

The thicker the string, the lower pitched the note.

How to read Tab.

A tab staff represents a guitar neck which has been laid on its side.

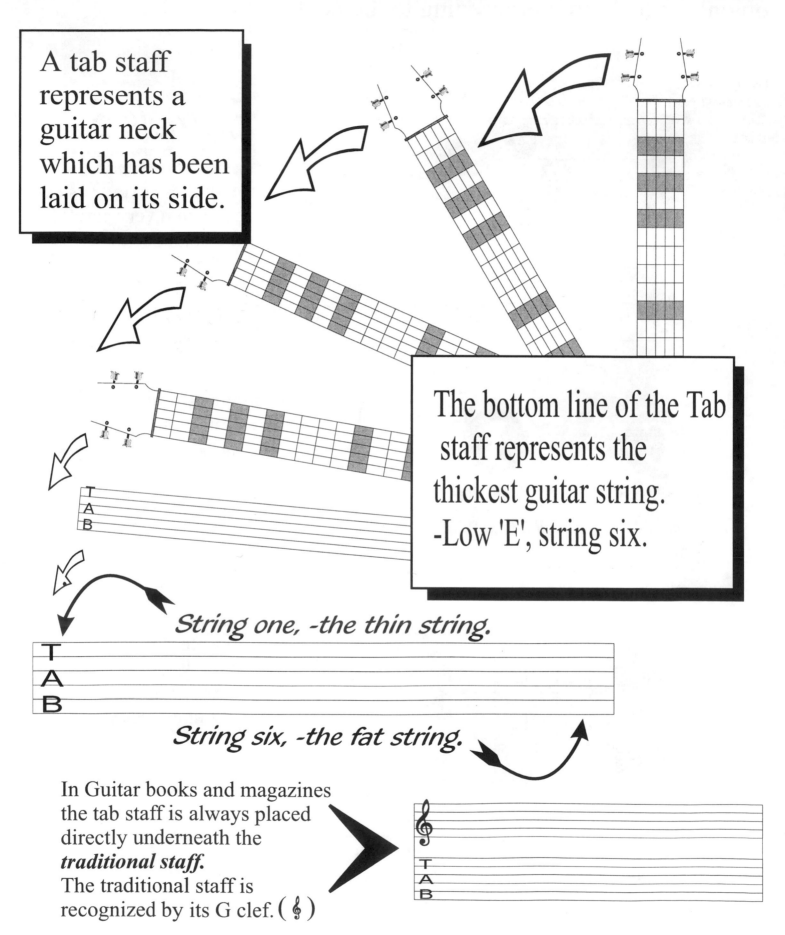

The bottom line of the Tab staff represents the thickest guitar string. -Low 'E', string six.

String one, -the thin string.

String six, -the fat string.

In Guitar books and magazines the tab staff is always placed directly underneath the *traditional staff.* The traditional staff is recognized by its G clef. (𝄞)

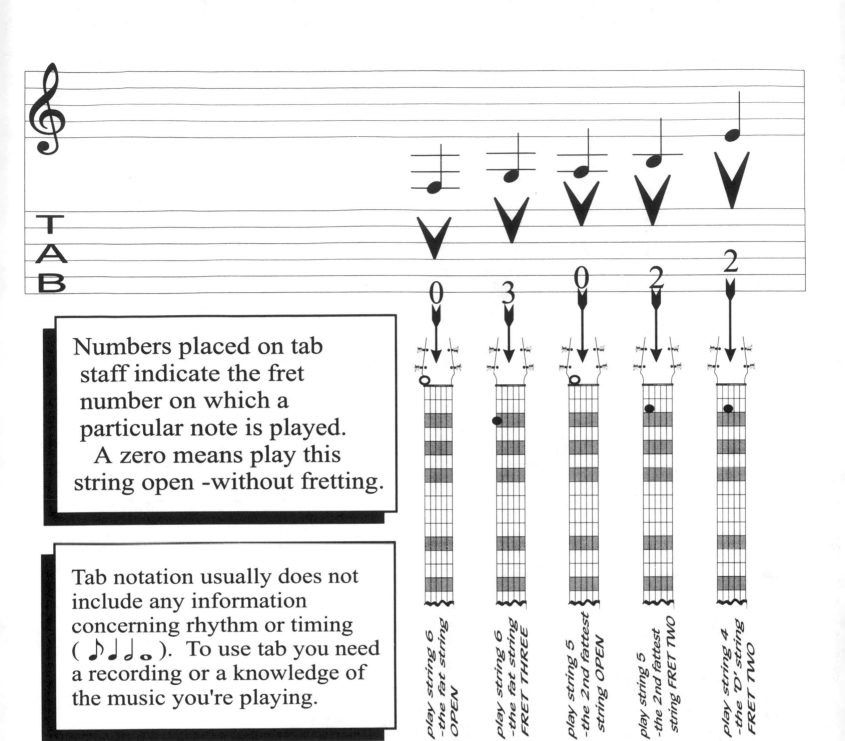

Numbers placed on tab staff indicate the fret number on which a particular note is played.
A zero means play this string open -without fretting.

Tab notation usually does not include any information concerning rhythm or timing (♪ ♩ ♩ 𝅝). To use tab you need a recording or a knowledge of the music you're playing.

play string 6 -the fat string OPEN

play string 6 -the fat string FRET THREE

play string 5 -the 2nd fattest string OPEN

play string 5 -the 2nd fattest string FRET TWO

play string 4 -the 'D' string FRET TWO

Musical Examples

Example 1

Example 2

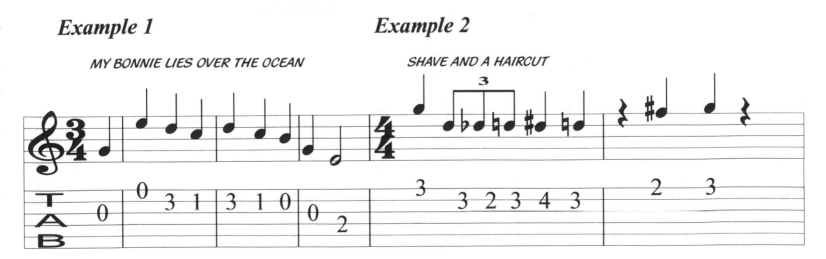

Playing in Position.

Guitar playing is thought about in reference to various positions. A *position* is a group of 4 frets. Each one of the frets in a *position* has a finger of the playing hand assigned to it.

For example, in the First Position *(Position I.)* all the notes in a scale or melody that were in the:

POSITION ONE

Open Strings

Fret One · Fret Two · Fret Three · Fret Four

I · II · III · IV

E B G D A E

1 2 3 4

1 2 3 4 5 6

EACH OF THE FIRST FOUR FRETS IS ASSIGNED IT'S OWN FINGER.

Playing Hand

First fret would be played by the *First finger*
Second fret would be played by the *Second finger*
Third fret would be played by the *Third finger*
Fourth fret would be played by the *Fourth finger*

Note;
All open string notes are included in the first position.

POSITION TWO

Any note in the...

Second fret is played by the First finger
Third fret is played by the Second finger
Fourth fret is played by the Third finger
Fifth fret is played by the Fourth finger

I · II · III · IV · V · VI

1 2 3 4

IN POSITION TWO...
STRETCH THE FIRST FINGER BACK TO PLAY THE FIRST FRET
STRETCH THE FOURTH FINGER UP TO PLAY THE SIXTH FRET

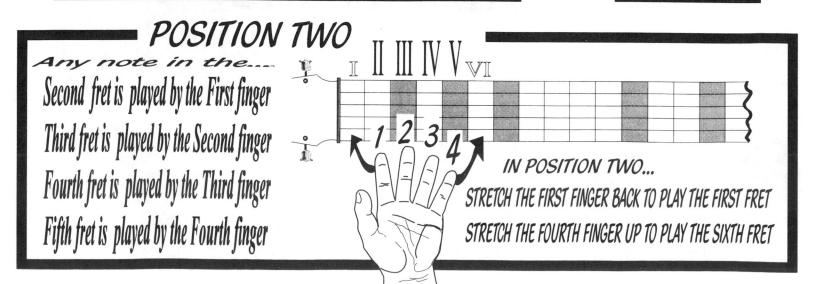

POSITION THREE

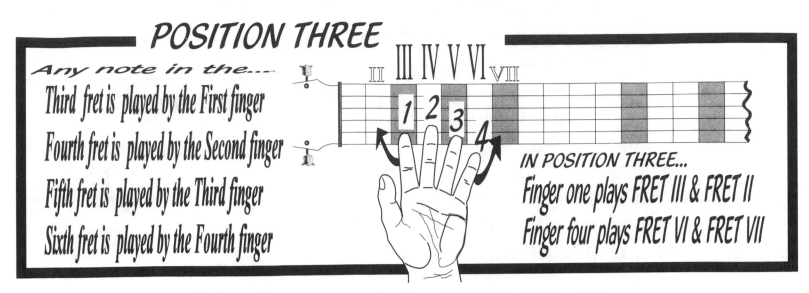

Any note in the...

Third fret is played by the First finger

Fourth fret is played by the Second finger

Fifth fret is played by the Third finger

Sixth fret is played by the Fourth finger

IN POSITION THREE...
Finger one plays FRET III & FRET II
Finger four plays FRET VI & FRET VII

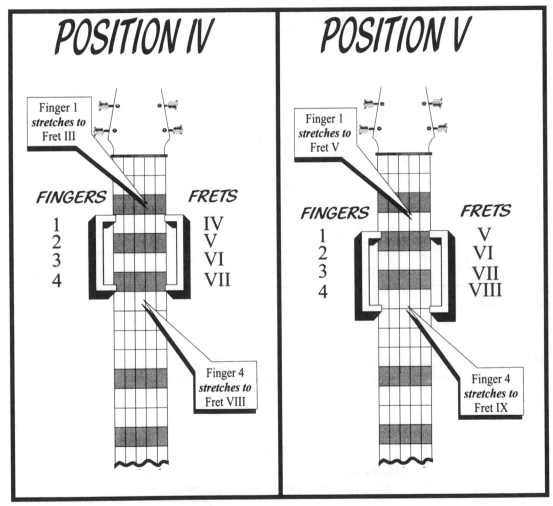

POSITION IV

Finger 1 *stretches to* Fret III

FINGERS
1
2
3
4

FRETS
IV
V
VI
VII

Finger 4 *stretches to* Fret VIII

POSITION V

Finger 1 *stretches to* Fret V

FINGERS
1
2
3
4

FRETS
V
VI
VII
VIII

Finger 4 *stretches to* Fret IX

IN ANY POSITION...

Each Finger is assigned its own fret.

Finger one can **stretch back** from its assigned fret, if needed.

Finger four can **stretch up** from its assigned fret, if needed.

Understanding the Musical Staff

To understand music theory, all guitarists must be acquainted with the traditional **Grand Staff** and how to name the notes on it. Study and refer to the charts below.

THERE ARE TWO CLEFS:

TREBLE

For the higher notes

BASS

For the lower notes

The Clefs are each placed on their own *Staff.*

Notes are placed on the various lines and spaces of the staff to indicate different pitches.

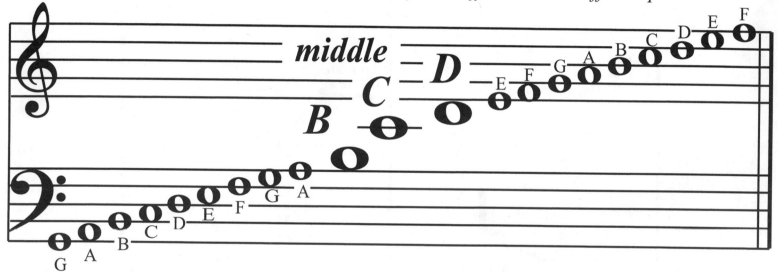

Notes too high or low to be on the staff are placed on *Ledger Lines.*

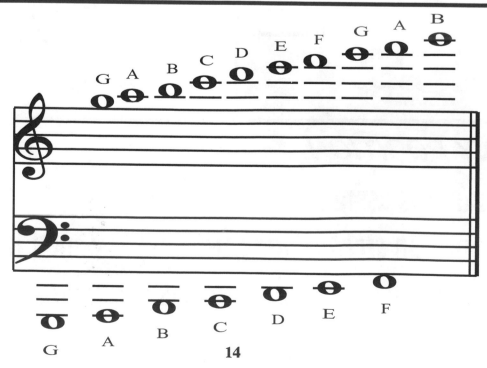

Musical notes for the bass and guitar are written in these *registers.*

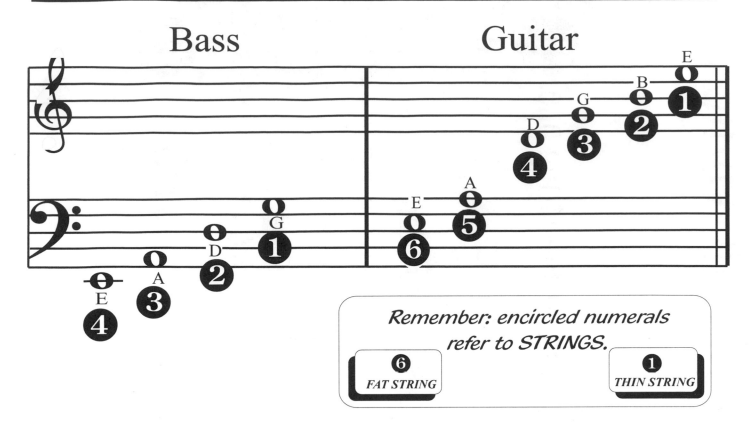

Bass

Guitar

Remember: encircled numerals refer to STRINGS.

⑥ FAT STRING

① THIN STRING

Guitar

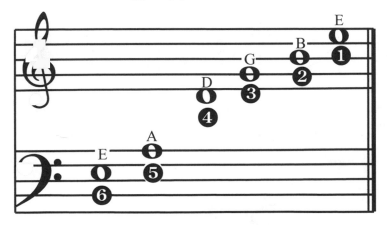

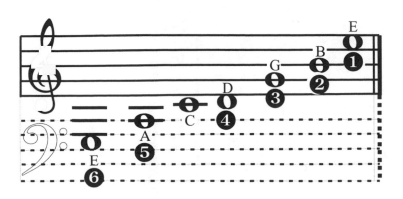

The illustration at left shows where written guitar notes fall on the Grand Staff.

Music for the guitar is always written in the *Treble Clef.* The lowest pitched notes, appearing on ledger lines, would actually fall in the bass clef of the *Grand Staff*.

The ledger lines, except for *Middle* "C", are really part of the *Bass Clef*.

15

The complete notes of the Guitar.

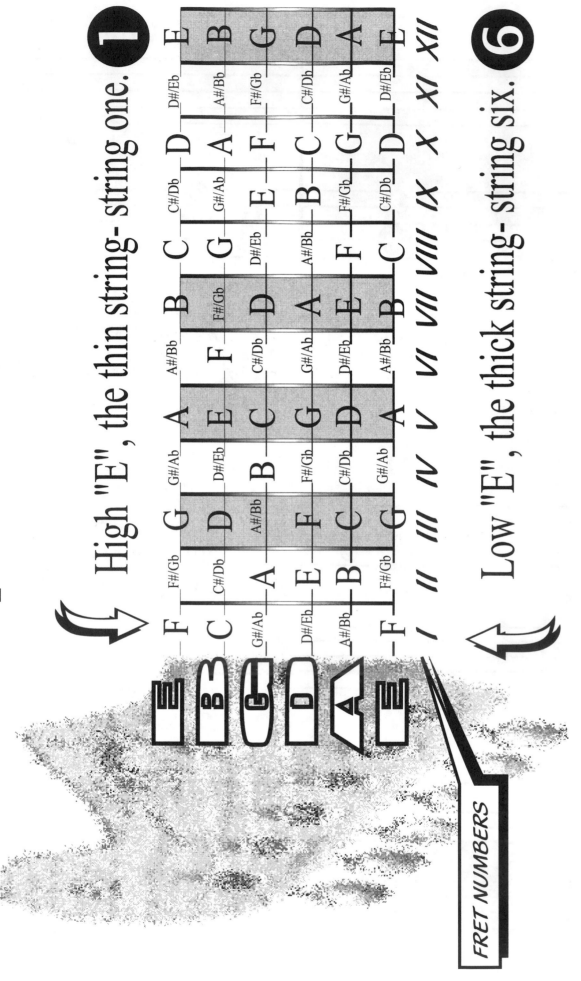

High "E", the thin string- string one.

Low "E", the thick string- string six.

FRET NUMBERS

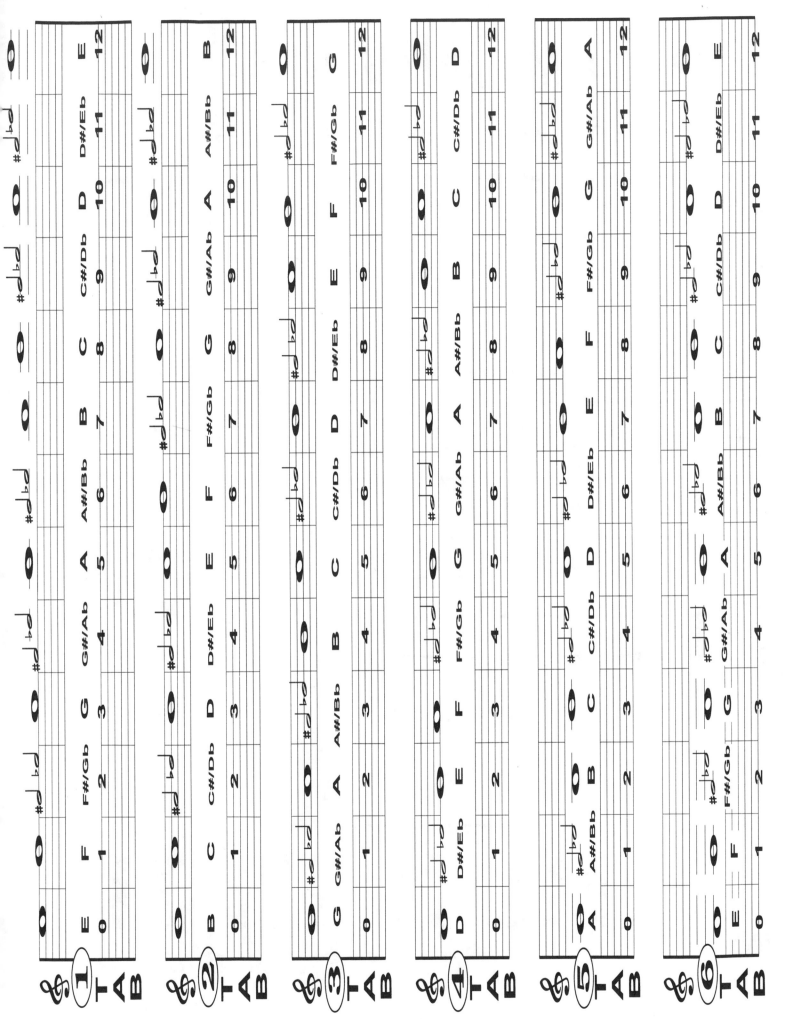

Key of: *C Major*

The key of C Major has No flats or sharps

1st Step- Play a C Major scale sliding up the second string. Make sure you can see the pattern & hear the sound of the scale. ⟹ *Do, Re, Mi, Fa, Sol, La, Ti, Do* ⟹

2nd Step- Starting on **Do**, play one octave of the C Major scale in the first position. Make sure you can see & hear the scale.

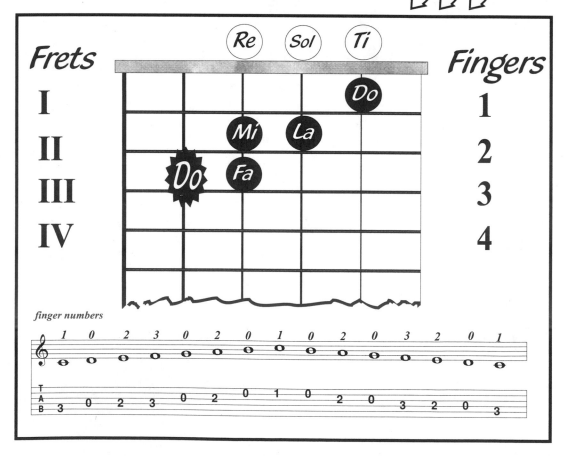

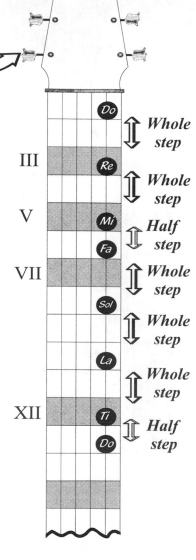

Whole step
Whole step
Half step
Whole step
Whole step
Whole step
Half step

Frets
I
II
III
IV

Re Sol Ti

Do
Mi La
Do Fa

Fingers
1
2
3
4

finger numbers

1 0 2 3 0 2 0 1 0 2 0 3 2 0 1

3rd step- Play one octave of the scale on your keyboard.

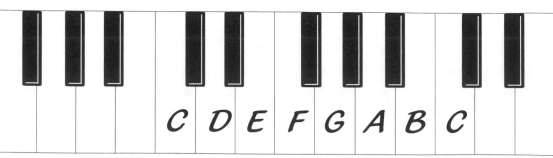

C D E F G A B C

Do	Re	Mi	Fa	Sol	La	Ti	Do
1 (w)	2 (w)	3 (½)	4 (w)	5 (w)	6 (w)	7 (½)	8
C	D	E	F	G	A	B	C

4th Step- Play some music using only notes from the scale. A simple melody like "TWINKLE, TWINKLE LITTLE STAR" should do nicely. Try to make up your own melody as well.

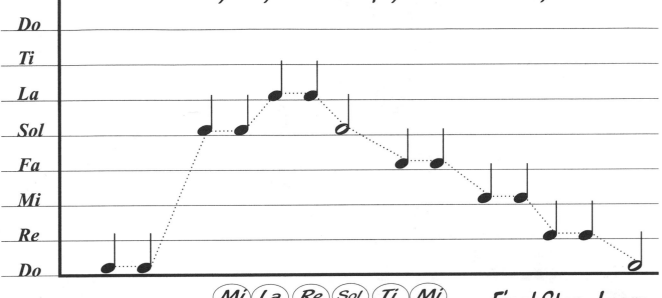

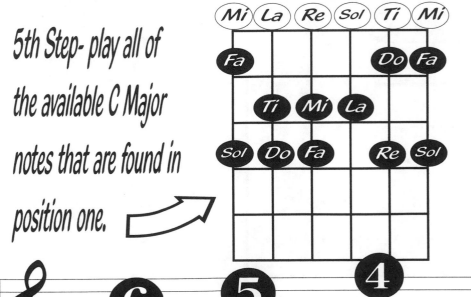

5th Step- play all of the available C Major notes that are found in position one.

Final Step- Learn how to play the C Major Scale by reading standard musical notation and TAB notation.

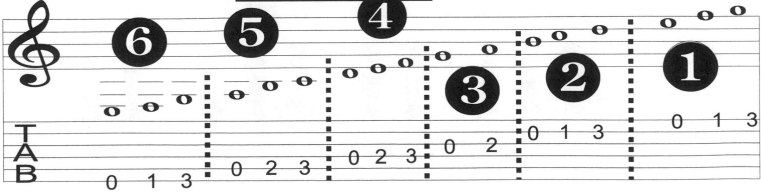

19

Key of: *G Major*

The key of G Major has ONE sharp: F#

1st Step- Play a G Major scale sliding up the third string
Make sure you can see the pattern & hear the
sound of the scale.

2nd Step- Play two octaves of G Major scale in the
first position. Make sure you can see
& hear the scale. Start on *Do* .

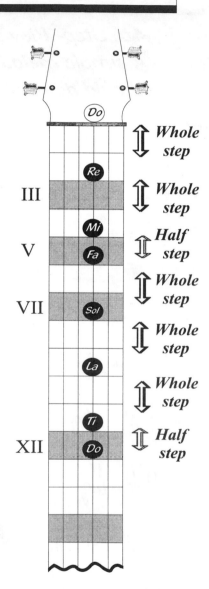

	Do	
III	*Re*	Whole step
		Whole step
V	*Mi*	Half step
	Fa	
VII		Whole step
	Sol	Whole step
	La	Whole step
	Ti	Whole step
XII	*Do*	Half step

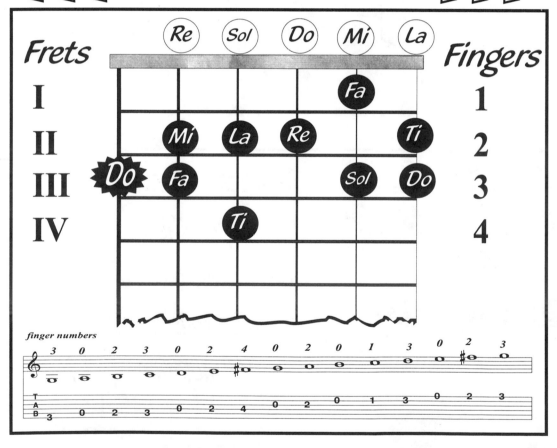

Frets

I
II
III
IV

Re *Sol* *Do* *Mi* *La*

Fa
Mi *La* *Re* *Ti*
Do *Fa* *Sol* *Do*
Ti

Fingers

1
2
3
4

finger numbers
3 0 2 3 0 2 4 0 2 0 1 3 0 2 3

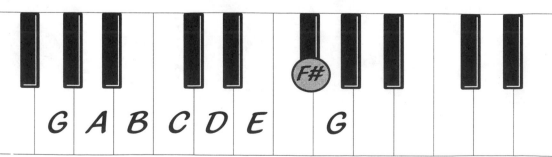

3rd step-
Play one octave
of the scale on
your keyboard.

F#

G A B C D E G

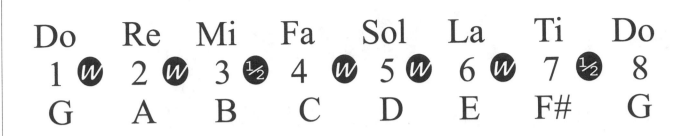

Do	Re	Mi	Fa	Sol	La	Ti	Do
1 (w)	2 (w)	3 (½)	4 (w)	5 (w)	6 (w)	7 (½)	8
G	A	B	C	D	E	F#	G

4th Step- Play some music using only notes from the scale. Re-learn "TWINKLE, TWINKLE LITTLE STAR" with this new scale. Playing the same tune with a different scale is called TRANSPOSING. Try to make up your own melody as well.

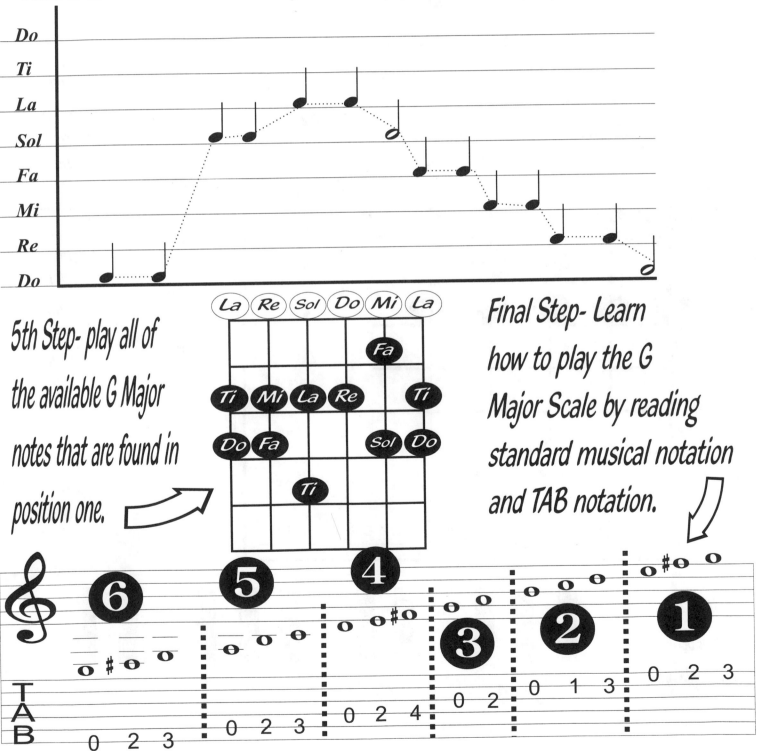

5th Step- play all of the available G Major notes that are found in position one.

Final Step- Learn how to play the G Major Scale by reading standard musical notation and TAB notation.

21

Key of: *F Major*

The key of F Major has ONE flat: Bb

1st Step- Play a F Major scale sliding up the FAT string
Make sure you hear the sound of the scale:
"Do, Re, Mi, Fa, Sol, La, Ti, Do."

2nd Step- Starting on **Do**, play two octaves of an F Major scale in the first position. Make sure you can see & hear the scale.

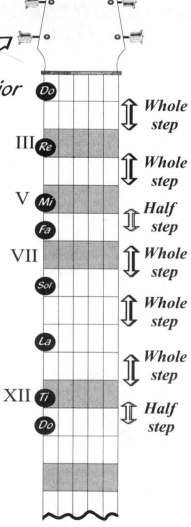

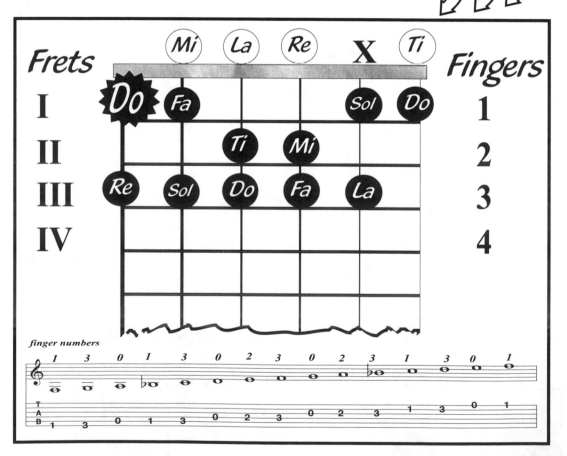

3rd step-
Play one octave
of the scale on
your keyboard.

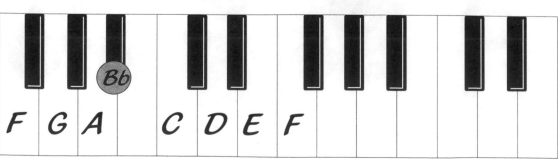

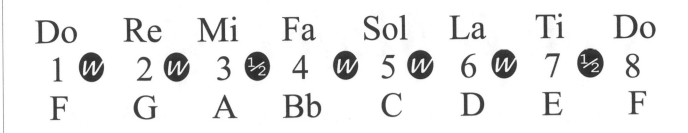

Do	Re	Mi	Fa	Sol	La	Ti	Do
1 (w)	2 (w)	3 (½)	4 (w)	5 (w)	6 (w)	7 (½)	8
F	G	A	Bb	C	D	E	F

4th Step- Play some music using only notes from the scale. Try out "FRERE JAQUES" as I have written below. Make up your own melody with the F MAJOR scale, trying to mentally 'hear' the notes prior to playing.

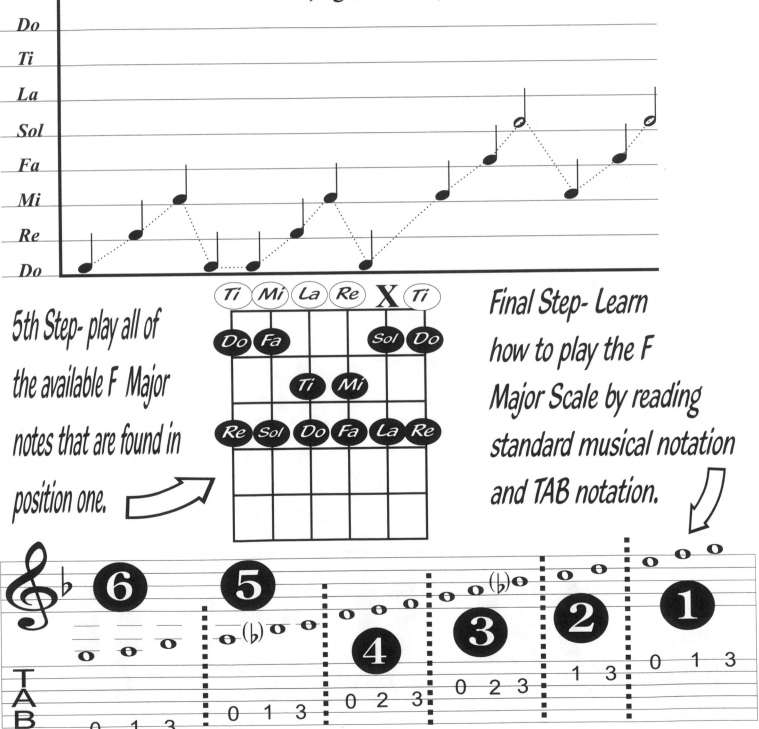

5th Step- play all of the available F Major notes that are found in position one.

Final Step- Learn how to play the F Major Scale by reading standard musical notation and TAB notation.

Key of: *D Major*

The key of D Major has TWO sharps: C# & F#

1st Step- Play a D Major scale sliding up the fourth string
Make sure you can see the pattern & hear
"Do, Re, Mi, Fa, Sol, La, Ti, Do".

2nd Step- Play one octave of the D Major scale in the
first position. Make sure you can see
& hear the scale. Start on Do.

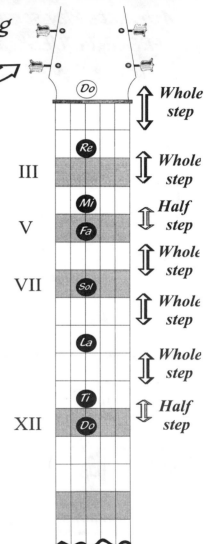

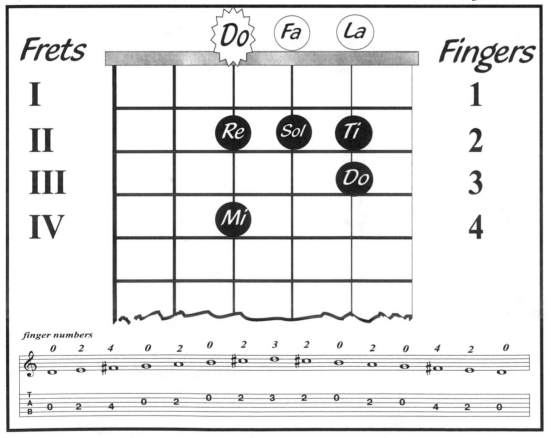

3rd step-
Play one octave
of the scale on
your keyboard.

Do	Re	Mi	Fa	Sol	La	Ti	Do
1 (w)	2 (w)	3 (½)	4 (w)	5 (w)	6 (w)	7 (½)	8
D	E	F#	G	A	B	C#	D

4th Step- Play some music using only notes from the scale. This time try "ROW, ROW, ROW YOUR BOAT". Of course, noodle around with the D MAJOR scale as you complete the tune by ear.

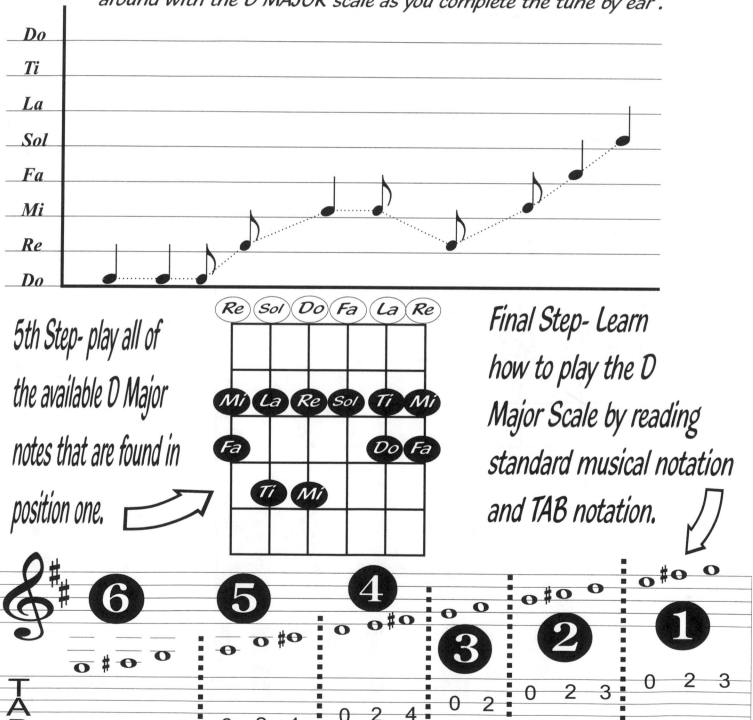

5th Step- play all of the available D Major notes that are found in position one.

Final Step- Learn how to play the D Major Scale by reading standard musical notation and TAB notation.

Key of: *Bb Major*

The key of Bb Major has TWO flats: Bb & Eb

1st Step- Play a Bb Major scale sliding up the fifth string
Be sure and train your ear to hear
"Do, Re, Mi, Fa, Sol, La, Ti, Do."

2nd Step- Play one octave of the Bb Major scale in the
first position starting on **Do** .
Be able to see & hear the scale.

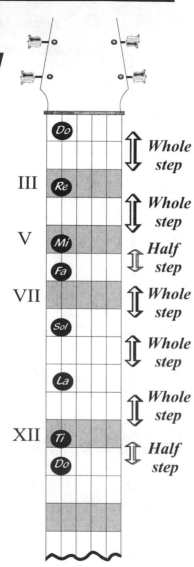

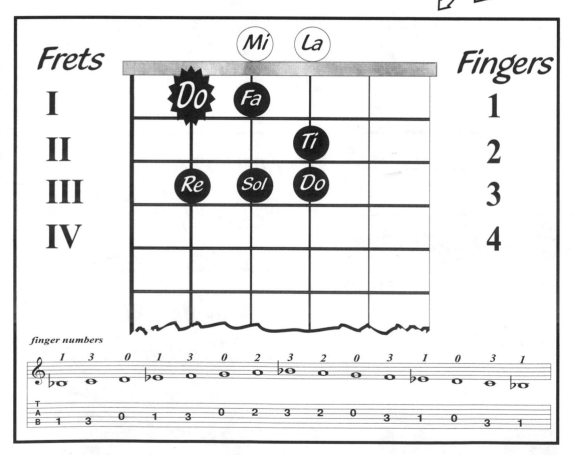

3rd step-
Play one octave
of the scale on
your keyboard.

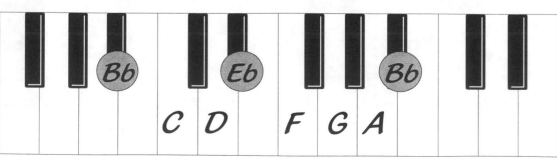

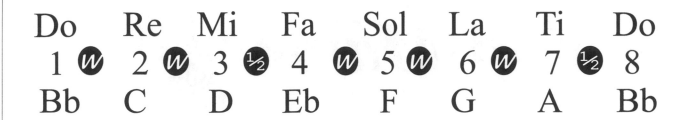

Do	Re	Mi	Fa	Sol	La	Ti	Do
1 (W)	2 (W)	3 (½)	4 (W)	5 (W)	6 (W)	7 (½)	8
Bb	C	D	Eb	F	G	A	Bb

4th Step- Play some music using only notes from the scale. Play "THE FIRST NOEL". Of course, noodle around with the Bb MAJOR scale as you compose your own tune.

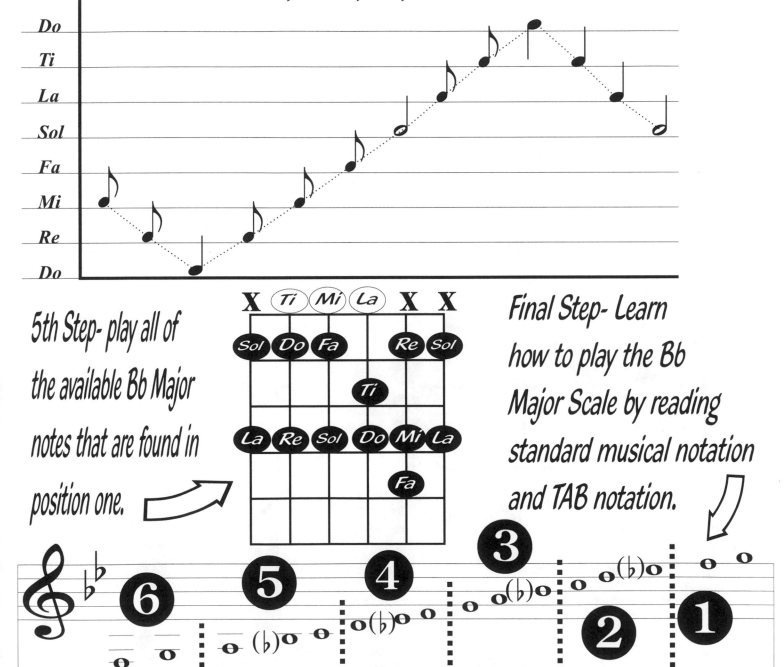

5th Step- play all of the available Bb Major notes that are found in position one.

Final Step- Learn how to play the Bb Major Scale by reading standard musical notation and TAB notation.

27

Key of: *A Major*

The key of A Major has THREE sharps: C#, F# & G#

1st Step- Play an A Major scale sliding up the fifth string.

2nd Step- Play two octaves of the A Major scale in the FIRST position. Starting on *Do*, see & hear the Scale.

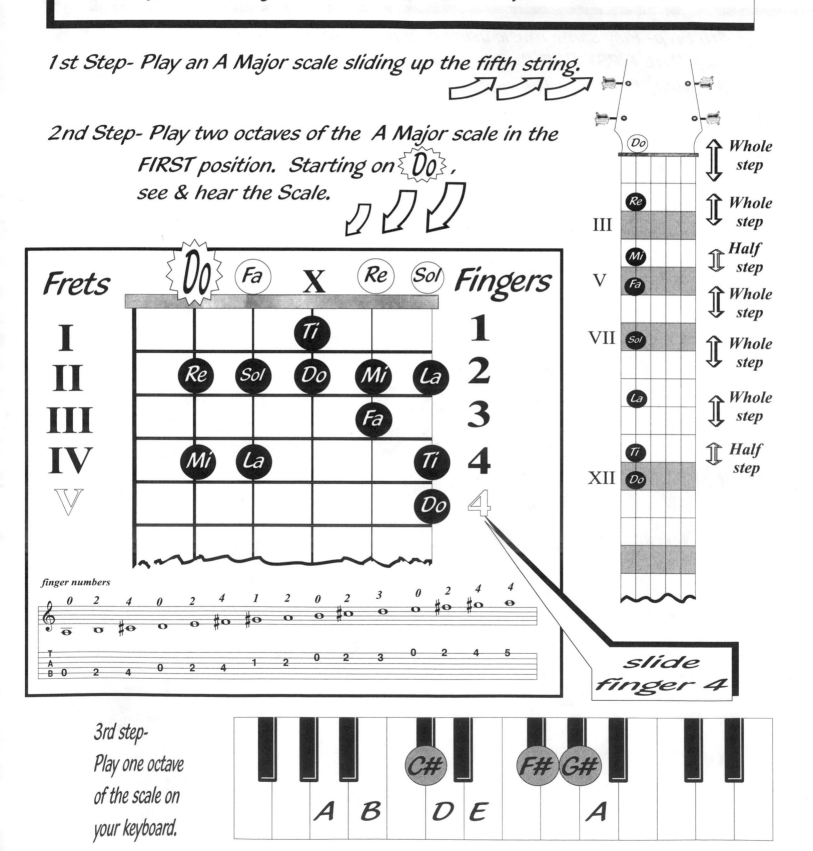

3rd step-
Play one octave
of the scale on
your keyboard.

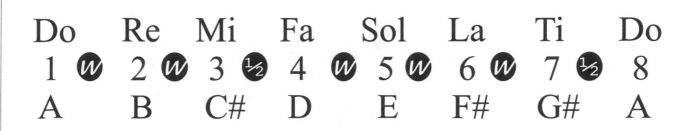

4th Step- Play some music using only notes from the scale.
"FOR HE'S A JOLLY GOOD FELLOW" is a great common knowledge melody
-nice and easy. The A MAJOR scale is a favorite among composing guitarists.

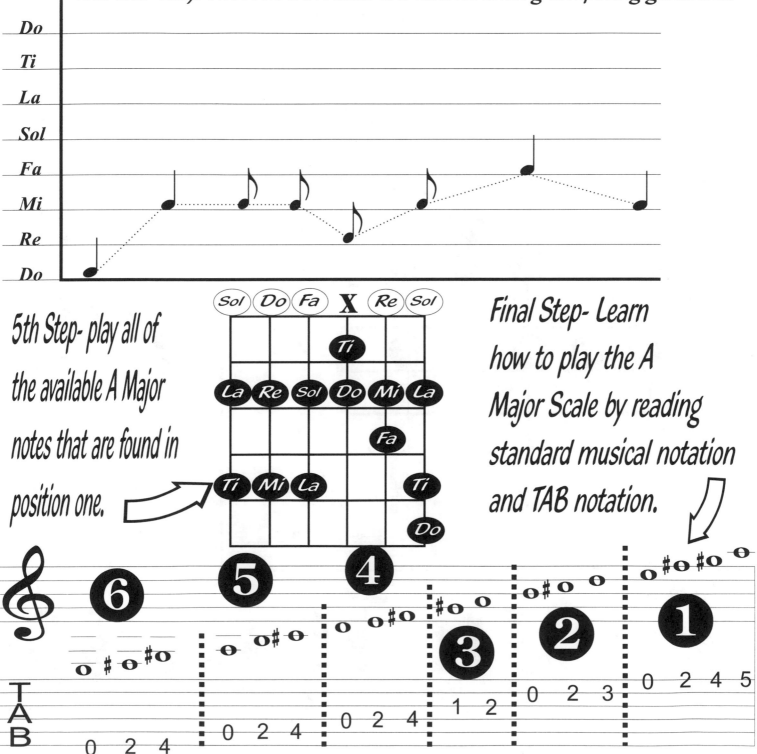

5th Step- play all of the available A Major notes that are found in position one.

Final Step- Learn how to play the A Major Scale by reading standard musical notation and TAB notation.

Key of: *E Major*

The key of E Major has FOUR sharps: F#, C#, G# & D#

1st Step- Play an E Major scale sliding up the sixth string.

2nd Step- Play two octaves of the E Major scale in the First position. Start on Do. Learn to hear the scales sound and visualize the pattern.

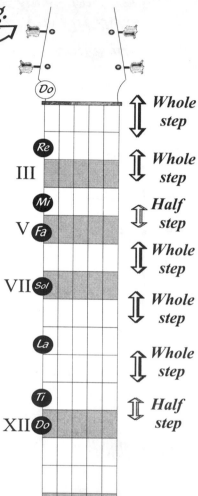

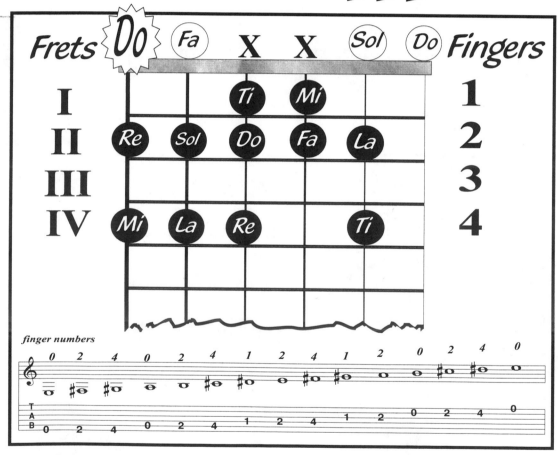

3rd step-
Play one octave
of the scale on
your keyboard.

Do	Re	Mi	Fa	Sol	La	Ti	Do
1 (w)	2 (w)	3 (½)	4 (w)	5 (w)	6 (w)	7 (½)	8
E	F#	G#	A	B	C#	D#	E

4th Step- Play some music using only notes from the scale. Pick out the "BRAHMS LULLABY". As with all the tunes we've studied so far, complete the tune using the trial and error process of playing by ear.

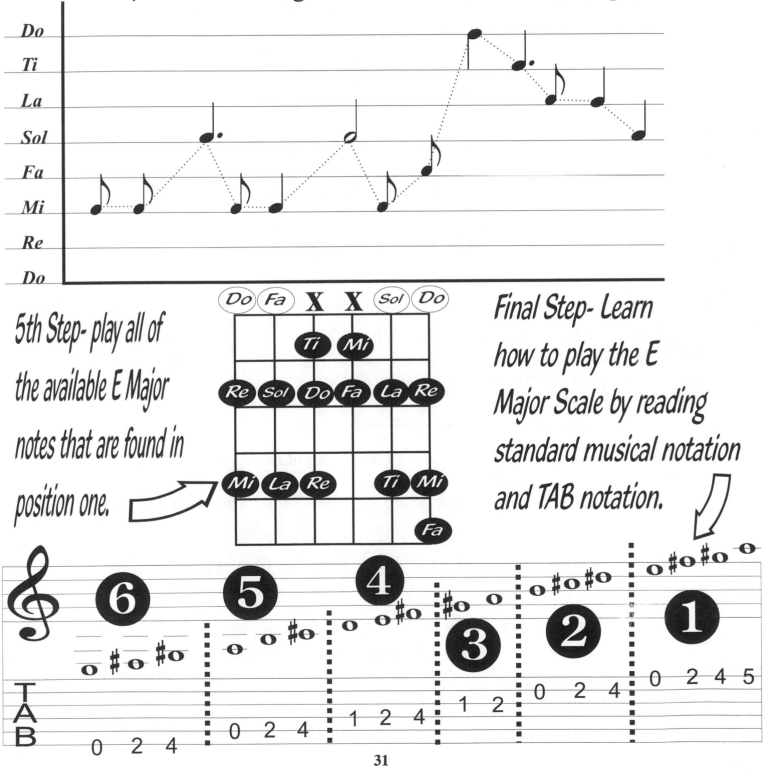

5th Step- play all of the available E Major notes that are found in position one.

Final Step- Learn how to play the E Major Scale by reading standard musical notation and TAB notation.

Musical Alphabet- A, B, C, D, E, F &G.
Every note in music has one of these seven names.

Flats and Sharps- Sometimes, two adjacent
notes have another note separating them. These are called
"flats and sharps". Think of as them as the **"black keys"** on a piano.
  Notice how the black keys can have either one of two names. The note
A SHARP is the same as **B FLAT**, **G SHARP** is the same as **A FLAT**.

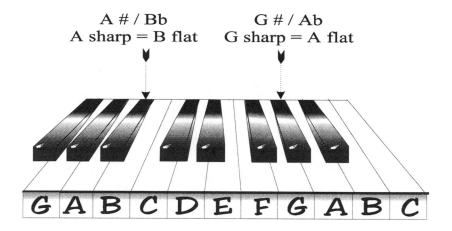

**SYMBOLS FOR SHARPED, FLATTED
OR NATURAL NOTES:**
*(Natural notes are the same as normal notes- ones that have not
been flatted or sharped)*

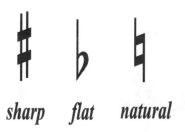

sharp   flat   natural

Chromatic Scale -The name given to **all of the notes** (flats, sharps and
naturals) when they are played or written for one octave, in order. The chromatic
Scale has 12 notes. The notes of a scale are often refered to as *'degrees'.*

A *A#/Bb* **B C** *C#/Db* **D** *D#/Eb* **E F** *F#/Gb* **G** *G#/Ab* **A**

*Important: The notes B & C do not share a flat/sharp note.
The notes E & F do not share a flat/sharp note.*

Half Step- Is the name given to a distance of one degree *(one note)* of the chromatic scale. This distance (or *"interval"*) separating any two adjacent notes is called a **HALF STEP**. For example, from **F# to G** or from **C# to D** as illustrated below.

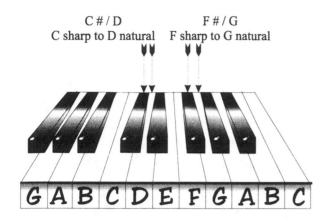

Whole Step- The name given to a distance of two degrees *(two notes)* of the chromatic scale. This distance, or *interval*, of two half steps is called a **WHOLE STEP**. For example, from **G to A** or from **F# to G#** as illustrated below.

Octave-Two notes separated by 12 degrees *(half steps)* of the chromatic scale have the same name. One of the notes is exactly twice as high in pitch as the other note. These two notes are said to be *an octave apart*.

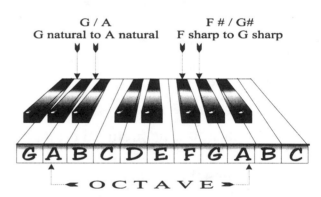

On the guitar, all the frets are separated by a distance of a **half step**. Each fret is equal to one note *(degree)* of the chromatic scale.

Half Step.   Whole Step.   Octave.

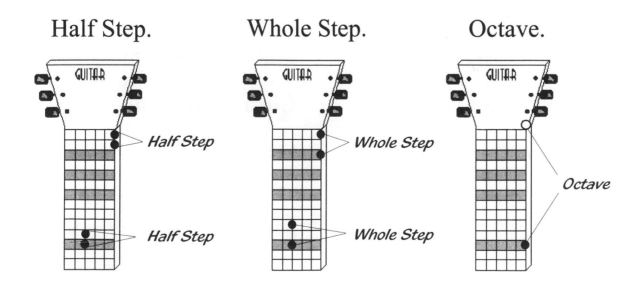

33

🔑 Every single note on the guitar can be given a letter name taken from the *chromatic scale*:

A *A#/Bb* **B** **C** *C#/Db* **D** *D#/Eb* **E** **F** *F#/Gb* **G** *G#/Ab* **A**

🔑 The open strings, for example, have the following names:

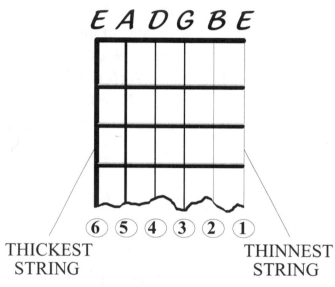

THICKEST STRING

THINNEST STRING

🔑 If you know the exact letter names of the **open stings** and you understand that each fret of the guitar is equal to one degree of the **chromatic scale** it's easy to figure out the exact letter name of any note

on your guitar as pictured on page 38.

🔑 In order to *really play* and understand the Pop, Rock and Blues guitar you must know the **exact letter name** of each and every note on *string six* and *string five*.

Review:

Discuss the following with a friend or teacher:

Musical Alphabet   **Flats and Sharps**

Natural notes   **Chromatic Scale**

Half Step   **Octave**

Whole Step

♯ ♭ ♮

String six
String five

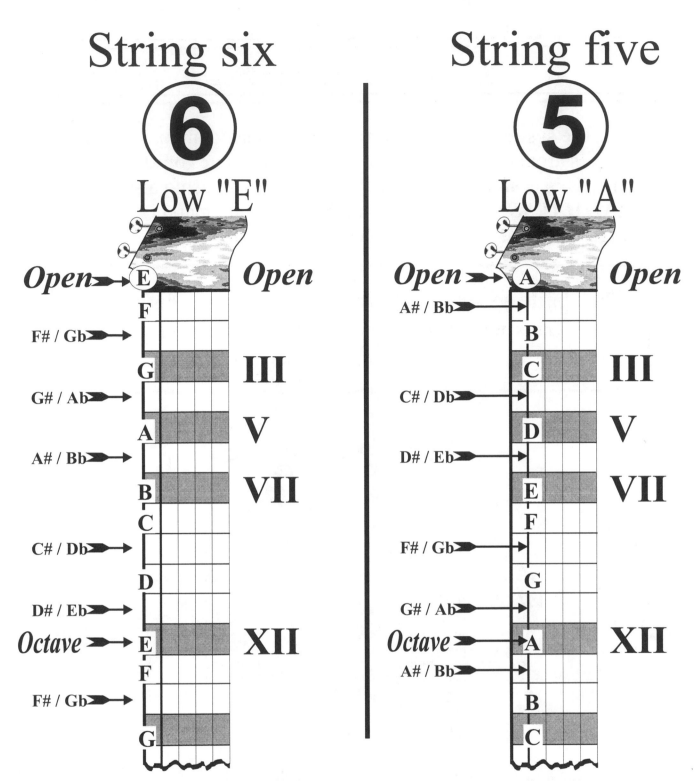

The name of an open string and the name of the note on the 12th fret of that string are exactly the same -only an octave apart.

Notice the large roman numerals (**III**, **V**, **VII** and **XII**). These are the frets that have position markers ("dots") on most guitars. Memorize the names of those notes first (on frets **III**, **V**, **VII** and **XII**) and use them as reference points while playing, learning and practicing.

Call frets **III**, **V**, **VII** and **XII** the *LANDMARKS*.

Root 6 & Root 5 Thinking.

The system of guitaristic thinking presented in this book revolves around memorizing the names of the notes on strings 6 and 5. This is **absolutely critical**. I've suggested using a system of *LANDMARKS* which correspond to the position markers *("dots")* found on frets **III, V, VII**, and **XII** on most guitars .

The shadings on our guitar neck diagrams reflect the frets which are thought of as landmarks.
(frets III, V, VII, and XII)

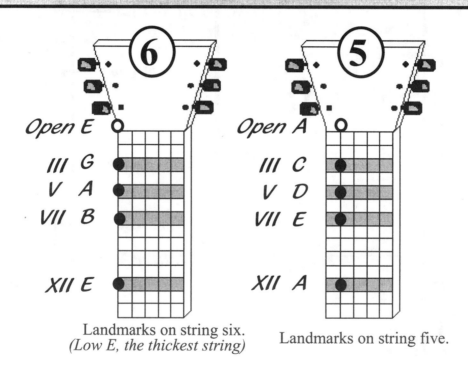

Landmarks on string six.
(Low E, the thickest string)

Landmarks on string five.

Each and every note in the chromatic scale,

A	A#/Bb	B	C	C#/Db	D	D#/Eb	E	F	F#/Gb	G	G#/Ab	A

is important in the playing of and thinking about music. The exercises on the opposite page will help you to develop the **crucial ability** to quickly name any note on the two thickest strings- low "E" and low "A". Write in the note names in the space above each guitar neck and check your work against the answers on the bottom of the page.

Note Naming Exercise

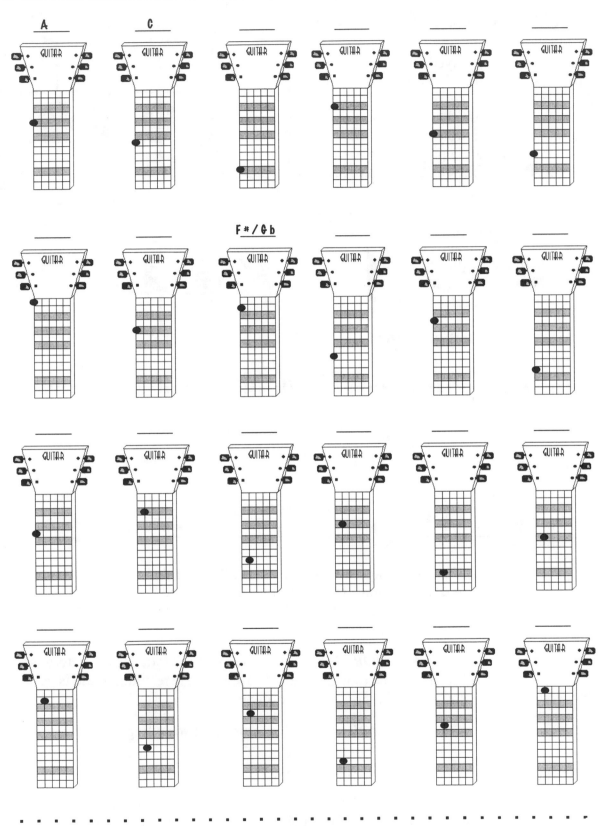

The Movable Root 6 Major Scale.

G Major Scale: Root Six

The most widely played and known form of a Major scale is illustrated at right. The Root note (*Do*), located on string six is the most important note in the scale. This is the note that names the scale and the note you think of first should you have occasion to play the scale.

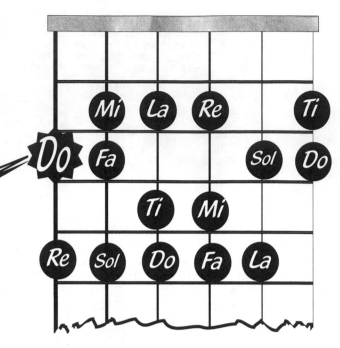

Do — *Root note*, 'G', string six is the first note played when practicing the scale. Start and end your practicing of the scale on this note. *(see tab)*

G Major Scale in Standard and Tab notation: Position II

The diagram at left contains **all available** G Major scale notes in the third position. The *'new'* notes are indicated with an arrow ( ).

On page 22 you see the same form of the scale relocated in three positions on the neck:

A MAJOR : When this same exact scale fingering pattern is played with the root note (*Do*) on fifth fret the resulting scale is an *A MAJOR SCALE* in the fourth position.

B MAJOR : When this same exact scale fingering pattern is played with the root note (*Do*) on the seventh fret the resulting scale is a *B MAJOR SCALE* in the sixth position.

E MAJOR : When this same exact scale fingering pattern is played with the root note (*Do*) on the twelfth fret the resulting scale is an *E MAJOR SCALE* in the eleventh position.

> THIS IS CALLED A ROOT SIX MOVABLE SCALE PATTERN, POSITION II

Root 6 A Major Scale, position IV

Root note -string six fret V. Finger one plays all notes on fret IV
Finger two plays root note (**Do**).

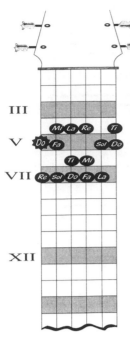

Do *Root note is "A" string* **⑥** *fret V*

Root 6 B Major Scale, position VI

Root note -string six fret VII. Finger one plays all notes on fret VI
Finger two plays root note (**Do**).

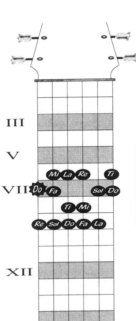

Do *Root note is "B" string* **⑥** *fret VII*

Root 6 E Major Scale, position XI

Root note -string six fret XII. Finger one plays all notes on fret XI
Finger two plays root note (**Do**).

Do *Root note is "E" string* **⑥** *fret XII*

The Movable Root 5 Major Scales.

C Major Scale: Root Five

A standard form of a movable Major scale is illustrated at right. The Root note (*Do*), located on string five is the most important note in the scale. This is the note that names the scale and the note you think of first should you have occasion to play the scale.

Do **Root note, "C" string 5 fret III.**
The starting and ending point for practicing the scale. In this version, the root is played with the second finger.

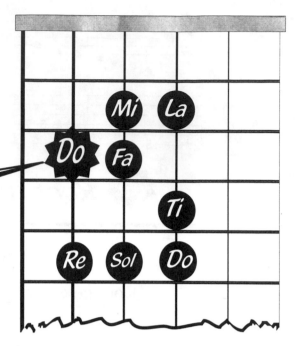

C Major Scale in Standard and Tab notation: Position II.

Extended C Major scale in Standard and Tab Notation: Position II.

The scale pattern below is a classic form of a C Major scale *(Root 5, position II)* which begins with finger 2 on the root (*Do*) and includes all possible notes in position II. The notes on fret one ("F" *stretch*) are to be played by stretching finger one **back one fret** out of position. Notes of fret II are also played by finger one. Notes on fret III are still to played as normal second position notes, that is with finger two.

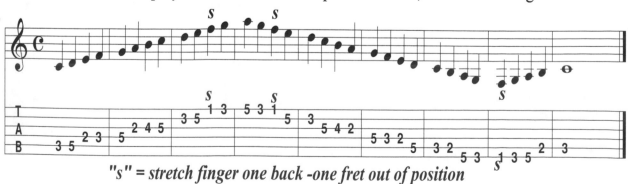

"s" = stretch finger one back -one fret out of position

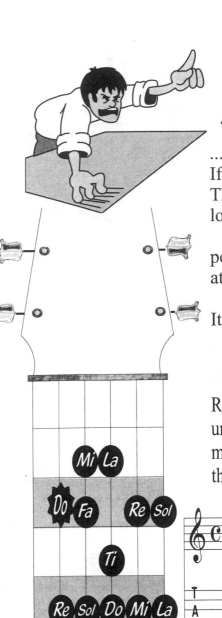

A Disagreement....

...often arises in any discussion of scales and their "correct" fingerings. If you think about it, how could any one such idea be **THE** right one? The point is that a series of notes has to be played comfortably and logically - the way you do it is your business.

Fortunately for guitar students, there are a lot of accomplished people in the same business. The various stratagies experts have arrived at are all worthy of study and evaluation.

The diagram at left is a multi position version of a Root 5 C Major scale. It's not the right way, its simply another very useful way.

Multi-position C scale favored by improvisers

Remember, regular Arabic numerals *(1,2,3,4)* refer to fingers of the fretting hand unless they appear on a tab staff - then the numbers refer to frets. As you read the music below, pay close attention to the fingering indications and the position shifts they cause.

Fingerings in bold italics.

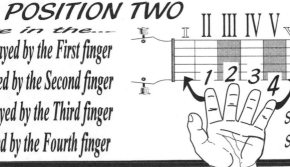

POSITION TWO

Any note in the...

Second fret is played by the First finger
Third fret is played by the Second finger
Fourth fret is played by the Third finger
Fifth fret is played by the Fourth finger

IN POSITION TWO...
STRETCH THE FIRST FINGER BACK TO PLAY THE FIRST FRET
STRETCH THE FOURTH FINGER UP TO PLAY THE FIFTH FRET

Root 5 C Major Scale, position II

Root note -string five, fret III. Finger one plays all notes on fret II *and* stretches back to play notes on fret I. Finger two plays root note (**Do**).

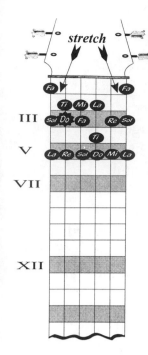

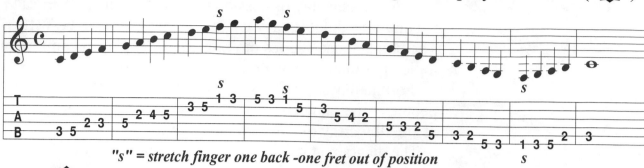

"s" = stretch finger one back -one fret out of position

Do Root note is "C" string ⑤ fret III

Root 5 D Major Scale, position IV

Root note -string five, fret V. Finger one plays all notes on fret IV *and* stretches back to play notes on fret III. Finger two plays root note (**Do**).

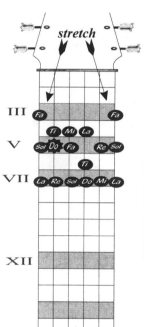

"s" = stretch finger one back -one fret out of position

Do Root note is "D" string ⑤ fret V

Root 5 E Major Scale, position VI

Root note -string five, fret VII. Finger one plays all notes on fret VI *and* stretches back to play notes on fret V. Finger two plays root note (**Do**).

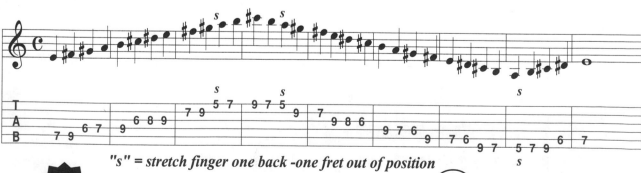

"s" = stretch finger one back -one fret out of position

Do Root note is "E" string ⑤ fret VII

Root 5 C Major Scale, multi-position

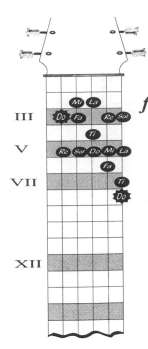

finger numbers

NOTE POSITION SHIFTS CAUSED BY FINGERING

Root 5 D Major Scale, multi-position

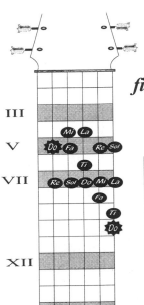

finger numbers

NOTE POSITION SHIFTS CAUSED BY FINGERING

Root 5 E Major Scale, multi-position

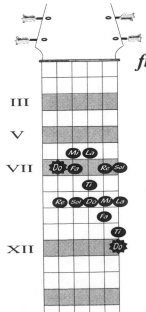

finger numbers

NOTE POSITION SHIFTS CAUSED BY FINGERING

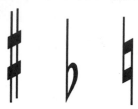 There are three types of notes:

All of which are derived from the Chromatic scale:

A *A#/Bb* **B C** *C#/Db* **D** *D#/Eb* **E F** *F#/Gb* **G** *G#/Ab* **A**

sharp   *flat*   *natural*

a 'natural' is a regular note
-one which <u>has not</u> been flatted or sharped.

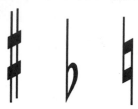 Any note in the chromatic scale *(sharp, flat or natural)*
can be the root note of a Major scale:

For Example:

A Major, Bb Major, B Major, C Major, Db Major, D Major, Eb Major, E Major,
F Major, Gb Major *(a.k.a. F# Major)*, **G Major, Ab Major.**

........the 12 possible Major scale names.

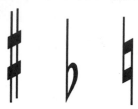 For *<u>any</u>* Major scale, we've learned how to play 2 versions:

Root 6   &   *Root 5*

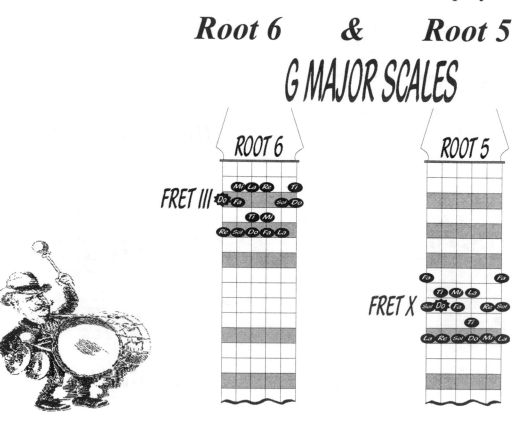

Music Theory: The Major Scale

The basis and foundation of music theory is the Major scale. The well known *sound* of the Major scale is that of **" Do Re Mi Fa Sol La Ti Do"**. All discussions of music theory are ultimately based on the Major scale.

Any of the scales in music derive their particular sounds from the distances separating their notes. This is called a *scale formula.* The chromatic scale *(see page 32)*, for example, has a distance of a half step between each one of its notes.

The formula for the chromatic scale is expressed as:
" half, half, half, half, half, half, half, half, half, half, half, half "

The formula for a Major scale is expressed as:
" whole, whole, half, whole, whole, whole, half "

The Major scale can be beautifully illustrated on one string of the guitar...

...or by playing only the white keys on a keyboard beginning and ending with "C".

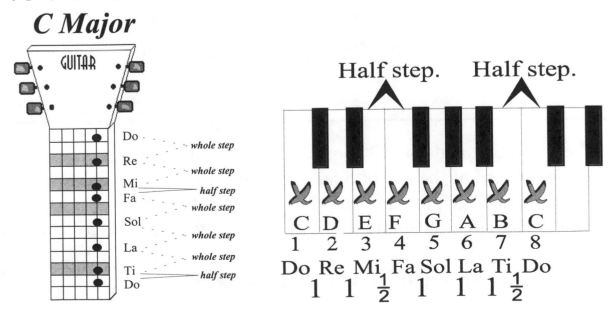

C Major

45

The formula for the major Scale is expressed as
"whole, whole, half, whole, whole, whole, half".

Any note in the chromatic scale can be the root of its own Major scale. It's possible to build twelve (and only twelve) separate and distinct Major Scales using the notes of the chromatic scale. Each new and unique Major scale is said to be a *"new key"*. There are twelve separate and distinct Major Scales and therefore **twelve keys** in the language of music.

Every 8 note major scale contains all seven letters of the musical alphabet with the first *(and last)* note of the scale being the **root note**. In order to play *(and hear)* a Major Scale starting on the "G", note we would first need the letters **"G A B C D E F G"**. According to the Scale formula the interval separating the last two notes must be a half step. That being the case, the type of "F" note we use must be an **"F#"**, not an **"F"**.

The correct *spelling* of a G Major scale is:

G A B C D E F# G

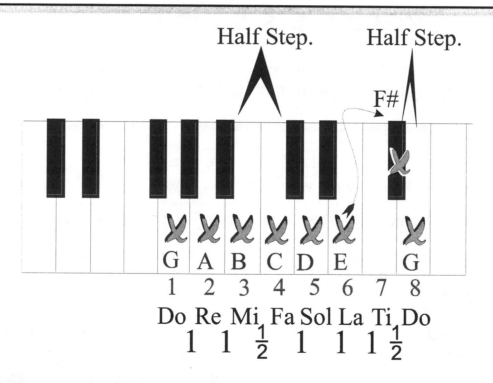

There is a demand for "F#" instead of "F natural" to preserve the formula **and sound** of the Major Scale. If you construct a major Scale with a root note of "G", there is one sharp needed **(F#)** in order to make it come out with the right sound. This is what is meant by the following statement:

"The key of G Major has one sharp"

One octave of *ANY MAJOR SCALE* contains eight notes. Half steps separate the 3RD and 4TH notes and also the 7TH and 8TH notes.

To construct a Major scale with a root note of "D", we first need to

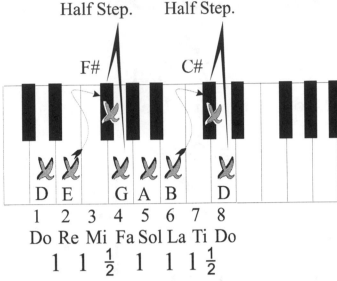

have these notes:

D E F G A B C D.

The *Major Scale formula* states that the interval separating notes **3&4** and also notes **7&8** must be a half step. That being the case, the type of "F" note we must use is **"F sharp"** and not **"F natural"**. Accordingly, type of "C" note we use is **"C Sharp"**, not **"C natural"**.

The correct *spelling* of a D Major scale is:

D E F# G A B C# D

Each new Major scale we construct is the basis of its own system of playing and composing called a *Key*.

The two keys we have studied so far *(the key of "D Major" & the key of "G Major")* are called *sharp keys* because they need to use sharped notes to have the correct formula -*and therefore sound* of their own, individual Major scale.

Flat Keys

Some keys need to use flatted notes to have the correct formula and sound of their own Major scale. They key of "F Major" is an example of a *flat key*.

To construct an F Major scale, we must start and end with a note of "F" and have every other letter of the musical alphabet represented once: **F G A B C D E F**. If the interval separating A & B (notes 3&4) must be a half step, the **"B"** note must then be flatted *(Bb)*. It's incorrect to call this note **"A#"** because a note named **"A"** is alreday included in the spelling.

The correct *spelling* of the F Major scale is:

F G A B*b* C D E F

Major Scale

Sharp Keys

1	2	3	4	5	6	7	8/1
Do	Re	Mi	Fa	Sol	La	Ti	Do

half step   *half step*

C	D	E	F	G	A	B	C	Key of C: *No Sharps*
G	A	B	C	D	E	F#	G	Key of G: *1 Sharp*
D	E	F#	G	A	B	C#	D	Key of D: *2 Sharps*
A	B	C#	D	E	F#	G#	A	Key of A: *3 Sharps*
E	F#	G#	A	B	C#	D#	E	Key of E: *4 Sharps*
B	C#	D#	E	F#	G#	A#	B	Key of B: *5 Sharps*
F#	G#	A#	B	C#	D#	E#	F#	Key of F#: *6 Sharps*

These **'sharp keys'** need to use sharped notes to create the sound of their own Major Scale.

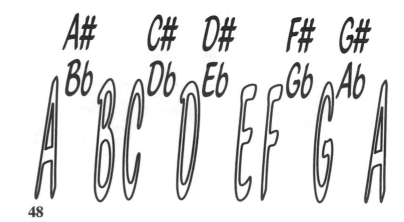

48

Reference Charts

Flat Keys

1	2	3	4	5	6	7	8/1
Do	Re	Mi	Fa	Sol	La	Ti	Do

half step   half step

C	D	E	F	G	A	B	C	Key of C: *No Flats*
F	G	A	Bb	C	D	E	F	Key of F: *1 Flat*
Bb	C	D	Eb	F	G	A	Bb	Key of Bb: *2 Flats*
Eb	F	G	Ab	Bb	C	D	Eb	Key of Eb: *3 Flats*
Ab	Bb	C	Db	Eb	F	G	Ab	Key of Ab: *4 Flats*
Db	Eb	F	Gb	Ab	Bb	C	Bb	Key of Db: *5 Flats*
Gb	Ab	Bb	Cb	Db	Eb	F	Gb	Key of Gb: *6 Flats*

Play a Major scale in every key.

write in every key

practice in every key

memorize these charts

| G | A | B | C | D | E | F | G | A | B | C |

These *'flat keys'* need to use flatted notes to create the sound of their own Major Scale.

49

Key: The Circle of Fifths

The diagram on the opposite page is **the** classic method of organizing the 12 keys in the language of Music. The inherent logic of this circle is very clearly evident when studying the two preceding pages of this book ('sharp keys' & 'flat keys').

When moving clockwise around the *circle of fifths*, the keys are separated by an *interval of a fifth*. That is to say **"G"** is the fifth note of a **"C"** Major scale while **"D"** is the fifth note of a **"G"** Major scale. I have clearly diagrammed this on page 48, entitled 'sharp keys'. When the keys are organized in this manner, each successive key contains **one more sharp** than the previous key. This is the logic and beauty of the *circle of fifths*.

When moving counter clockwise, the diagram is often called the *circle of fourths*. In this case, each new key contains <u>**one more flat**</u> than the previous key. The keys are separated by an interval of a fourth . This means **"F"** is the fourth note of a **"C"** Major scale while **"Bb"** is the fourth note of an **"F"** Major scale and so on. I've illustrated this idea on the page 49, entitled *'flat keys'*.

The circle of fifths is a systematic approach to organizing and memorizing the 12 keys of music according to the number of flats or sharps a key contains. All musicians must be totally comfortable with the circle of fifths.

E sharp & C flat

E sharp is another way of saying **F natural**. **C flat** is another way of saying **B natural**. These are called *enharmonic notes.*

The key of **F sharp** must contain a seventh note one half step lower than *"F#"*. Obviously this can't be called *"F"* because that would mean the scale could not be written correctly- the scale would have two types of *"F"* notes, *F sharp and F natural*. Therefore we must call the seventh note of an **F Sharp Major** scale *"E#"*.

The key of **G Flat** must contain a fourth note one half step higher than *"Bb"*. Obviously this can't be called *"B"* because that would mean **this** scale could not be written correctly- the scale would have two types of *"B"* notes, *B flat and B natural*. Therefore we must call the fourth note of a **G Flat Major** scale *"Cb"*.

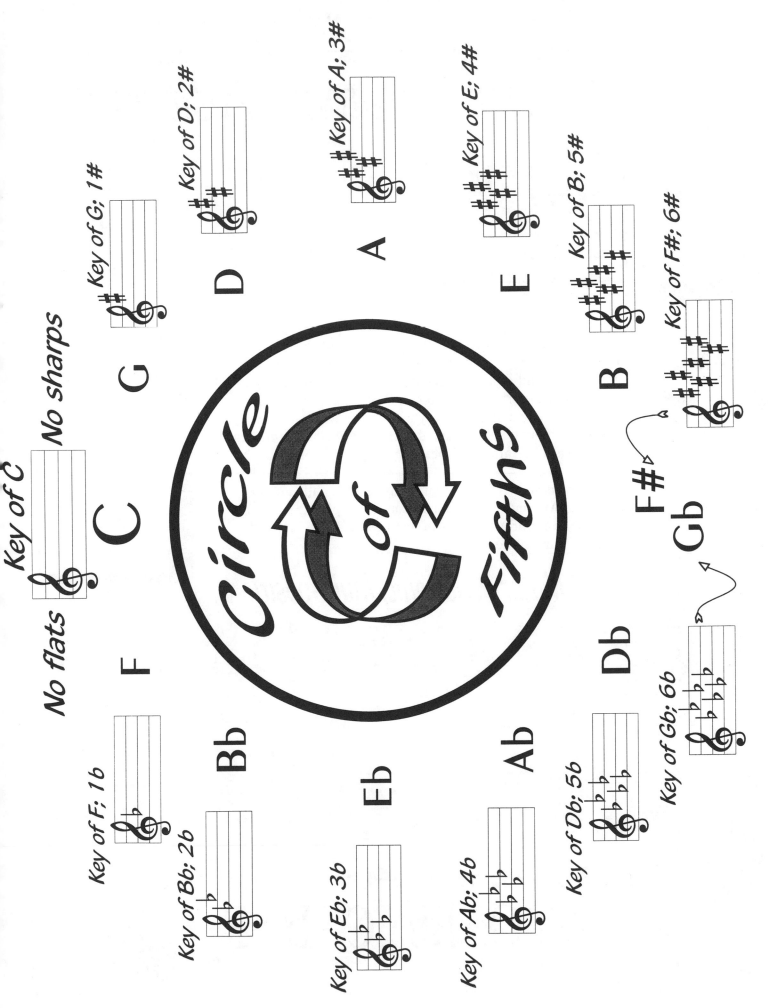

G Minor Pentatonic, Position III

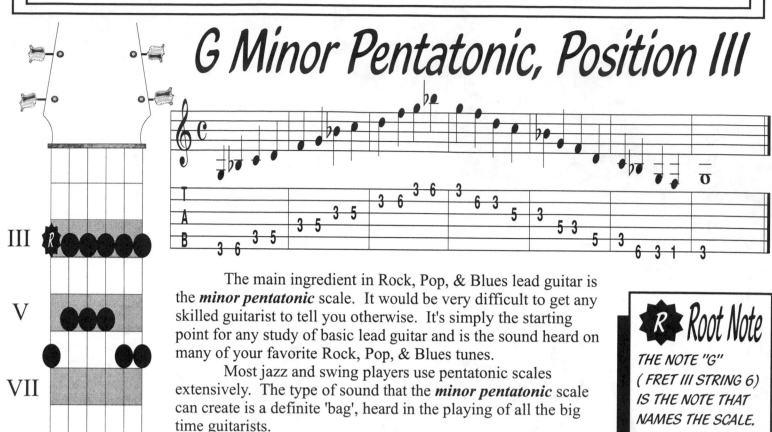

The main ingredient in Rock, Pop, & Blues lead guitar is the *minor pentatonic* scale. It would be very difficult to get any skilled guitarist to tell you otherwise. It's simply the starting point for any study of basic lead guitar and is the sound heard on many of your favorite Rock, Pop, & Blues tunes.

Most jazz and swing players use pentatonic scales extensively. The type of sound that the *minor pentatonic* scale can create is a definite 'bag', heard in the playing of all the big time guitarists.

Pentatonic scales are infinitely useful is all sorts of situations. Anyone serious about learning to play the guitar would make a thorough study of them while practicing and learning the instrument.

Root Note

THE NOTE "G" (FRET III STRING 6) IS THE NOTE THAT NAMES THE SCALE. THINK OF THIS NOTE FIRST WHEN LEARNING AND PRACTICING THE SCALE.

G Minor Pentatonic, Multi-position

G Minor Pentatonic

G MAJOR SCALE:
G A B C D E F# G
1 2 3 4 5 6 7 1

G ROOT **Bb** FLAT 3rd **C** FOURTH **D** FIFTH **F** FLAT 7th

G Blues Scale, Position III

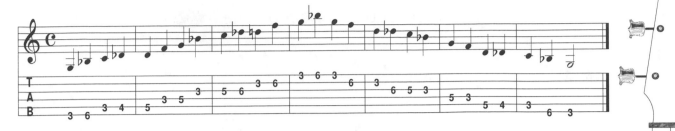

POSITION THREE

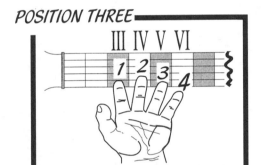

The sister scale of the Root 6 minor pentatonic scale is the Root 6 **Blues scale**. Many great recorded solos rely on the minor pentatonic and **Blues scales** for their sounds. Chuck Berry, B. B. King, Eric Clapton, Jimi Hendrix, Jimmy Page, Eddie van Halen, Robby Kreiger (*The Doors*), Howard Roberts, George Harrison, Carlos Santana, John Fogerty (*Credence*) and Joe Perry are a few guitarists known for their mastery of these rich and powerful scales.

Accomplished guitarists are careful not to let these two scales become the only tool in their arsenal. Playing (or **overplaying**) only one type of scale for every guitar solo is a terrible idea and a sure way to create a bland, lifeless style!

Its a mistake to discount the ***minor pentatonic*** and ***Blues scale*** as being amateurish and simplistic.

G Blues scale, Multi-position

Fingerings in
Bold Italics

G Blues scale

G	Bb	C	Db	D	F
ROOT	FLAT 3rd	FOURTH	FLAT FIVE	FIFTH	FLAT 7th

Root 6 A Minor Pentatonic Scale, position V

Root note -string six fret V. Finger one plays all notes on fret V
Finger one plays root note (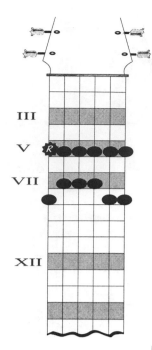 R).

 R *Root note is "A" string ⑥ fret V*

Root 6 B Minor Pentatonic Scale, position VII

Root note -string six fret VII. Finger one plays all notes on fret VII
Finger one plays root note (R).

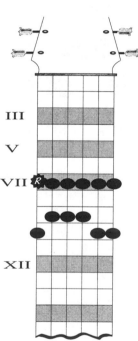

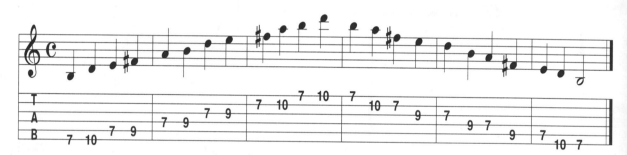

R *Root note is "B" string ⑥ fret VII*

Root 6 E Minor Pentatonic Scale, position XII

Root note -string six fret XII. Finger one plays all notes on fret XII
Finger one plays root note (R).

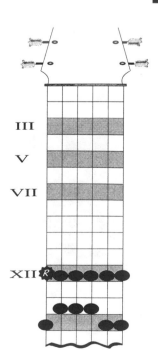

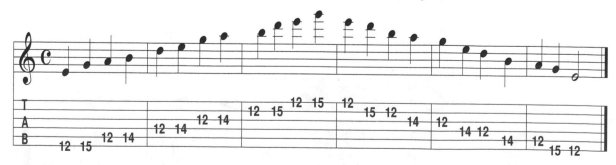

R *Root note is "E" string ⑥ fret XII*

Root 6 A Blues Scale, position V

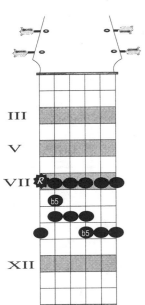

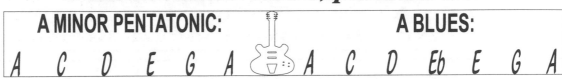

A MINOR PENTATONIC:						A BLUES:					
A	C	D	E	G	A	A	C	D	Eb	E	G	A

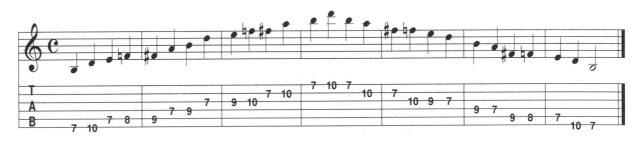

A MAJOR :

A B C# D E F# G# A

Root 6 B Blues Scale, position VII

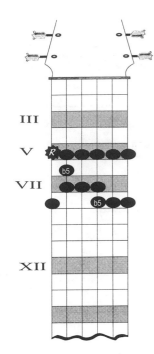

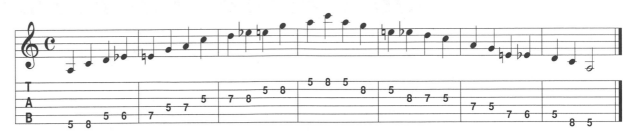

B MINOR PENTATONIC:						B BLUES:					
B	D	E	F#	A	B	B	D	E	F	F#	A	B

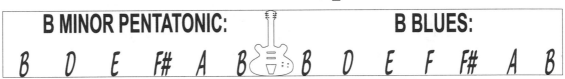

B MAJOR :

B C# D# E F# G# A# B

Root 6 E Blues Scale, position XII

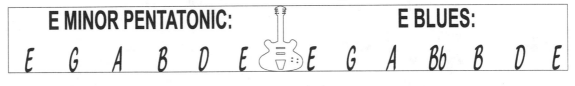

E MINOR PENTATONIC:						E BLUES:					
E	G	A	B	D	E	E	G	A	Bb	B	D	E

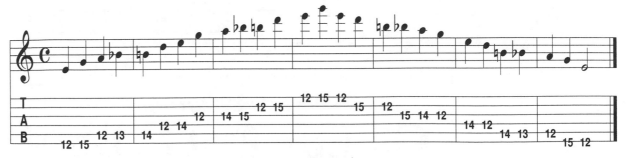

E MAJOR :

E F# G# A B C# D# E

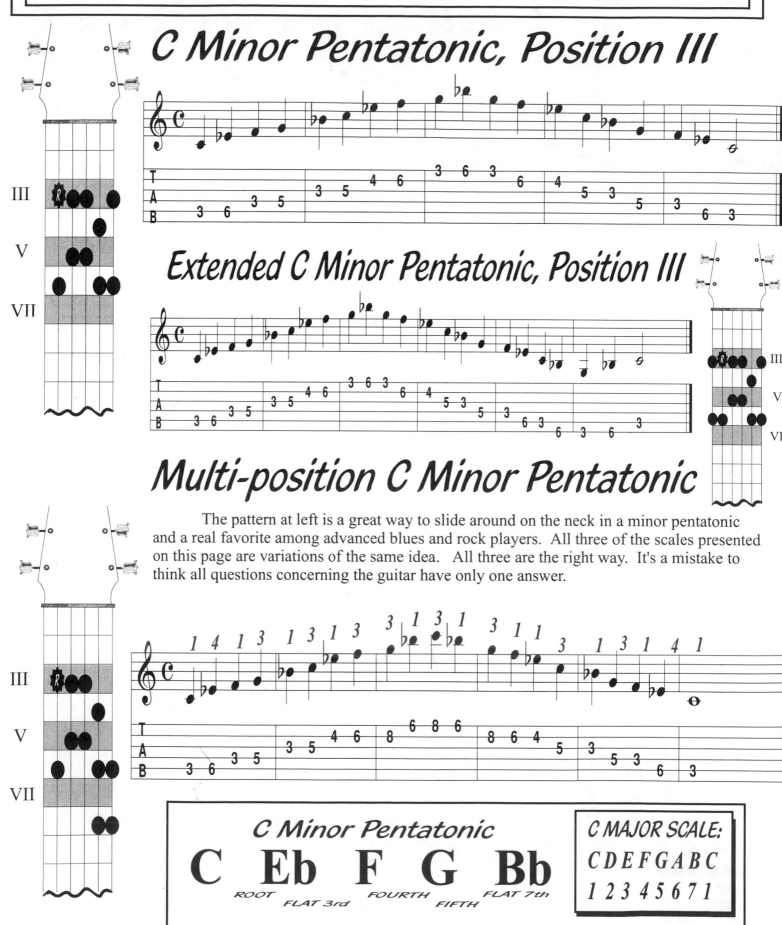

C Minor Pentatonic, Position III

Extended C Minor Pentatonic, Position III

Multi-position C Minor Pentatonic

The pattern at left is a great way to slide around on the neck in a minor pentatonic and a real favorite among advanced blues and rock players. All three of the scales presented on this page are variations of the same idea. All three are the right way. It's a mistake to think all questions concerning the guitar have only one answer.

C Minor Pentatonic

C   Eb   F   G   Bb

ROOT   FLAT 3rd   FOURTH   FIFTH   FLAT 7th

C MAJOR SCALE:

C D E F G A B C
1 2 3 4 5 6 7 1

C Blues Scale Position III

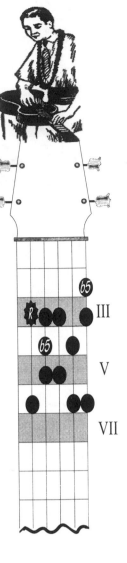

Fingerings in *Bold Italics*

Extended C Blues Scale, Position III

The 'extended' scales are those which contain every available scale tone in a particular position. I recommend that you always learn and practice any scale starting from the root note then progress to the extended scales.

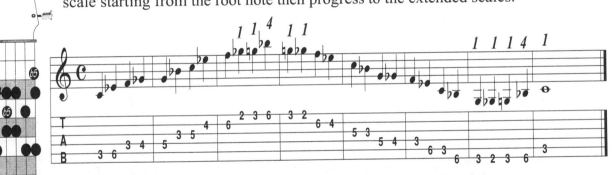

Multi-position C Blues Scale

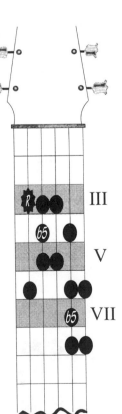

Any effective study of the guitar must address the issue of fingering. The multi-position scales I've suggested here are an excellent vehicle for learning to do this.

Mastering anything -a scale, riff, or entire piece is really a process of problem solving. The solution to any problem is usually developing a clever, elegant fingering to make what seemed impossible easy. This is how great guitarists develop that effortless quality to their playing.

Fingerings in *Bold Italics*

Root 5 D Minor Pentatonic Scale, position V

Root note -string five fret V. Finger one plays all notes on fret V
Finger one plays root note ().

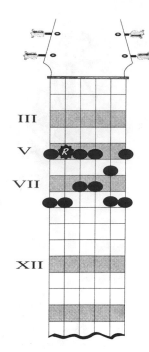

R *Root note is "D" string (5) fret V*

Root 5 E Minor Pentatonic Scale, position VII

Root note -string five fret VII. Finger one plays all notes on fret VII
Finger one plays root note (R).

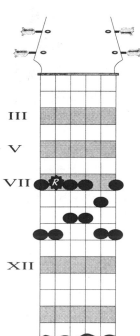

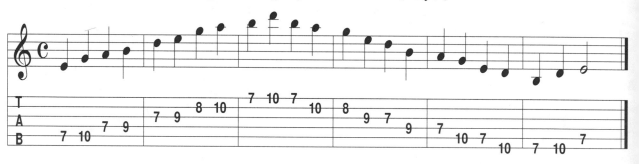

R *Root note is "E" string (5) fret VII*

Root 5 A Minor Pentatonic Scale, position XII

Root note -string six fret XII. Finger one plays all notes on fret XII
Finger one plays root note (R).

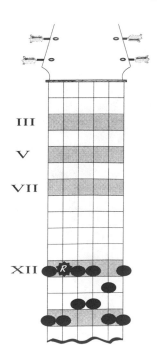

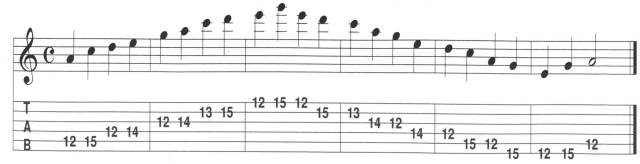

R *Root note is "A" string (5) fret XII*

58

Root 5 D Blues Scale, position V

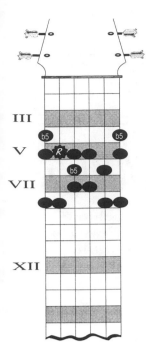

D MINOR PENTATONIC:							D BLUES:					
D	F	G	A	C	D		D	F	G	Ab	A	C	D

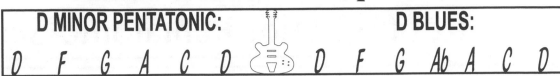

D MAJOR :

D E F# G# A B C# D

Root 5 E Blues Scale, position VII

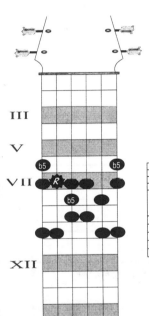

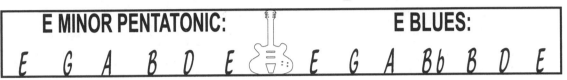

E MINOR PENTATONIC:							E BLUES:					
E	G	A	B	D	E		E	G	A	Bb	B	D	E

E MAJOR :

E F# G# A B C# E# E

Root 5 A Blues Scale, position XII

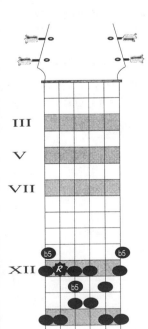

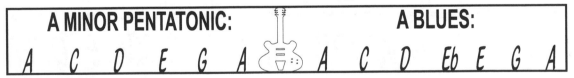

A MINOR PENTATONIC:							A BLUES:					
A	C	D	E	G	A		A	C	D	Eb	E	G	A

A MAJOR :

A B C# D# E F# G# A

G Major Pentatonic, Position II

The *Major pentatonic* scale at left is known for its sweet melodic quality. Robin Ford, B.B. King and Dickey Betts *(Allman Bros.)* are all associated with the sweet, tuneful sound of the *Major pentatonic* scale The root note is played with finger two since your first finger is assigned to fret II when playing in the second position.

SONGS WHICH USE THE MAJOR PENTATONIC SCALE

Blue Skies -Allman Bros.

Ramblin Man -Allman Bros

In A Sentimental Mood -Duke Ellington

Don't Worry, Be Happy -Bobby McFerrin

(opening phrase)

Breezin' -George Benson (solo section)

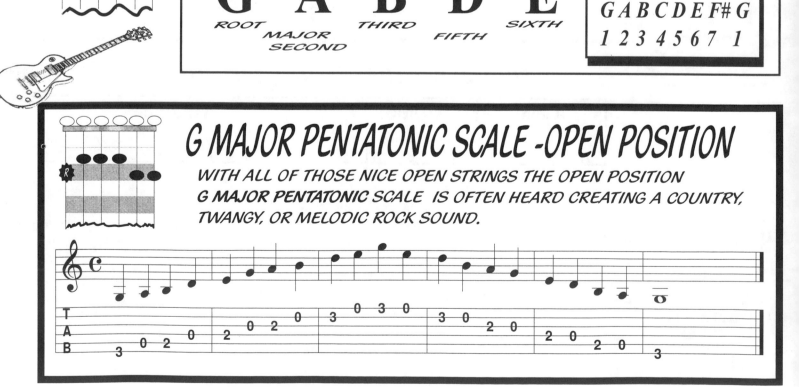

G Major Pentatonic

G A B D E

| ROOT | MAJOR SECOND | THIRD | FIFTH | SIXTH |

G MAJOR SCALE:
G A B C D E F# G
1 2 3 4 5 6 7 1

G MAJOR PENTATONIC SCALE -OPEN POSITION

WITH ALL OF THOSE NICE OPEN STRINGS THE OPEN POSITION G MAJOR PENTATONIC SCALE IS OFTEN HEARD CREATING A COUNTRY, TWANGY, OR MELODIC ROCK SOUND.

Multi-position G Major Pentatonic scale

The fingering for the multi-position pentatonic scale at right is one of the all-time cool guitar things. Using only the 1st and 3rd finger in a few comfortable slides enables you to easily cover the entire neck. Make sure you use the suggested fingering.

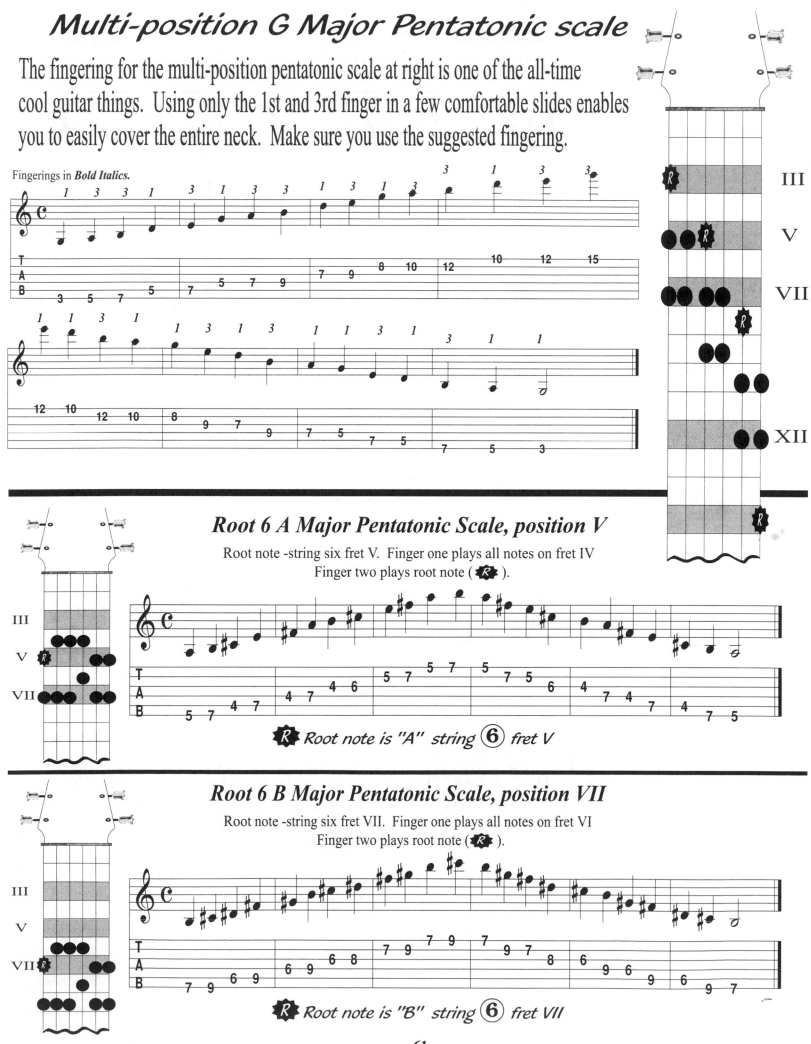

Fingerings in **Bold Italics.**

Root 6 A Major Pentatonic Scale, position V

Root note -string six fret V. Finger one plays all notes on fret IV
Finger two plays root note (R).

R Root note is "A" string ⑥ fret V

Root 6 B Major Pentatonic Scale, position VII

Root note -string six fret VII. Finger one plays all notes on fret VI
Finger two plays root note (R).

R Root note is "B" string ⑥ fret VII

61

Root 5 Major Pentatonic Scales

C Major Pentatonic, Position II

The root note is played with finger two since your first finger is assigned to the second fret when playing in the second position. The illustrations at left & right are the movable root 5 versions of the sweet and melodic Major pentatonic scale. Always begin & end practicing the C Major pentatonic scale on its root note, **"C"** *(string 5, fret III).*

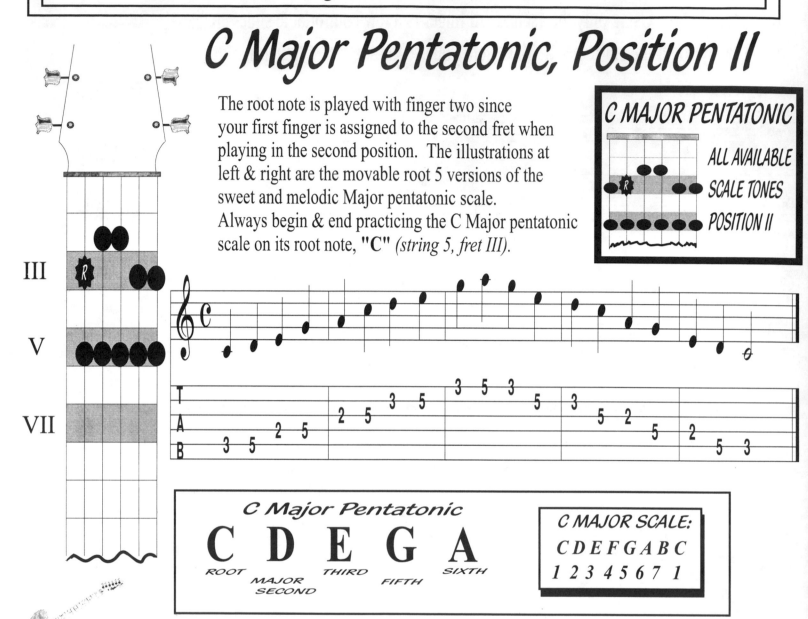

C MAJOR PENTATONIC
ALL AVAILABLE
SCALE TONES
POSITION II

III
V
VII

C Major Pentatonic

C D E G A

ROOT
MAJOR SECOND
THIRD
FIFTH
SIXTH

C MAJOR SCALE:
C D E F G A B C
1 2 3 4 5 6 7 1

C MAJOR PENTATONIC SCALE -OPEN POSITION

THIS OPEN POSITION SCALE IS ALSO GREAT FOR COUNTRY AND MELODIC ROCK AND ROLL. MAKE SURE TO BEGIN AND END YOUR PRACTICING WITH THE ROOT NOTE AS ILLUSTRATED BELOW.

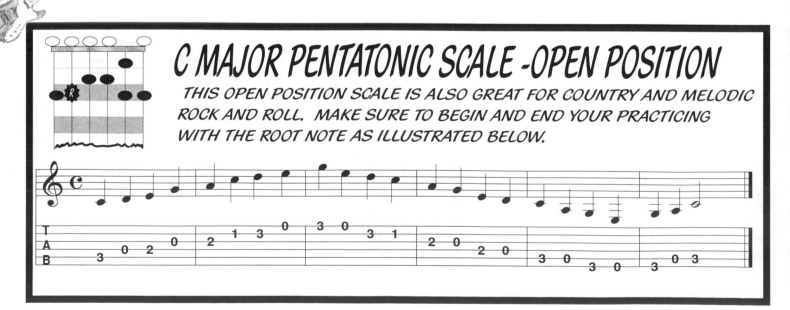

Multi-position C Major Pentatonic scale

Here is another must know sliding version of the *Major pentatonic.* Its ease of fingering and wide sonic range make it a favorite among guitarists.

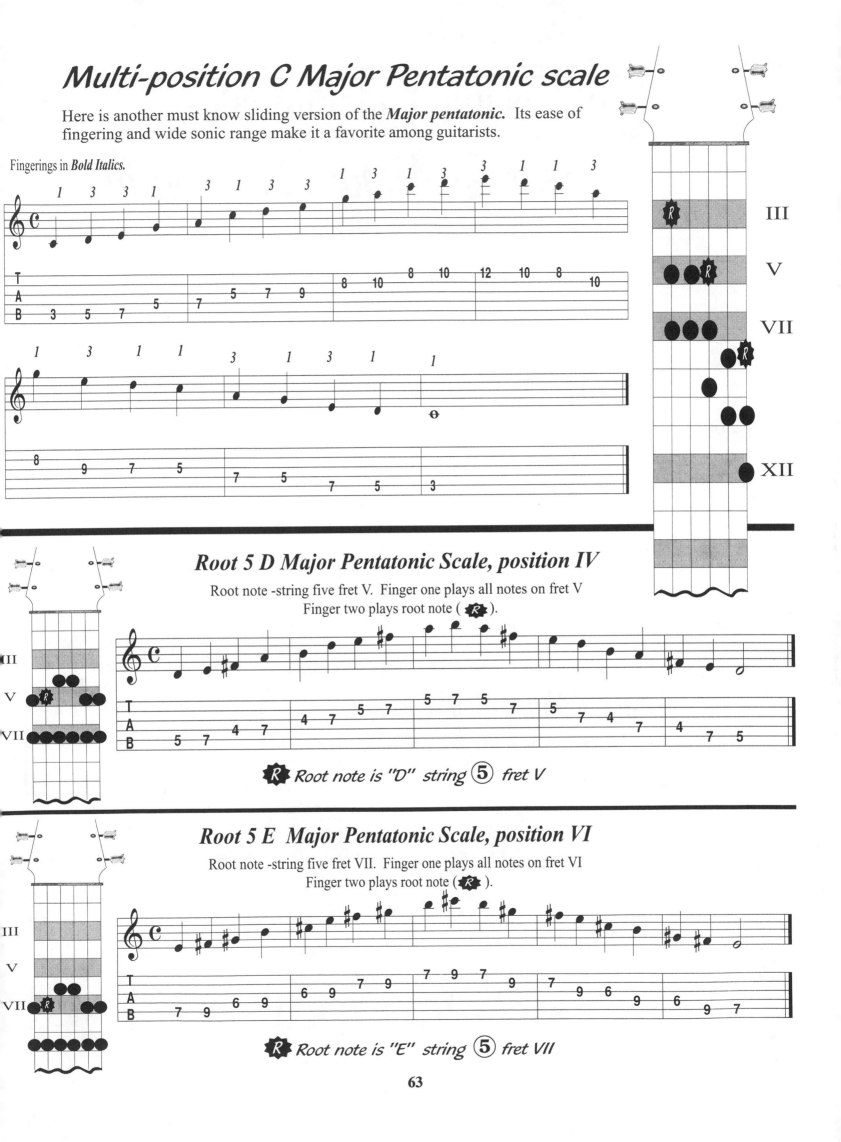

Fingerings in *Bold Italics.*

Root 5 D Major Pentatonic Scale, position IV

Root note -string five fret V. Finger one plays all notes on fret V
Finger two plays root note (R).

R Root note is "D" string ⑤ fret V

Root 5 E Major Pentatonic Scale, position VI

Root note -string five fret VII. Finger one plays all notes on fret VI
Finger two plays root note (R).

R Root note is "E" string ⑤ fret VII

G Natural Minor, Position III

Ascending

String 4

stretch finger 4

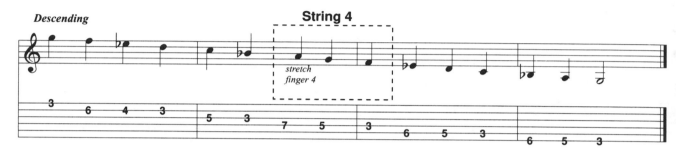

Descending

String 4

stretch finger 4

The one note on the seventh fret (A natural) is played with an out of position stretch of finger four. Its a little awkward at first but has a nice, thick feel and texture to it.

The multi-position option illustrated below, *(also "the right way")* is thought of as a 'speed' fingering.

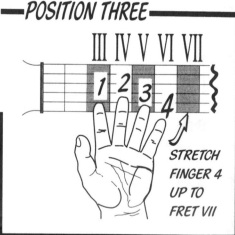

— POSITION THREE —

III IV V VI VII

1 2 3 4

STRETCH FINGER 4 UP TO FRET VII

G Natural Minor, Multi-position

The variation illustrated below requires two slight position shifts: *from position III to II, then and back to position III.* The notes A, Bb & C notes are located on string 2.

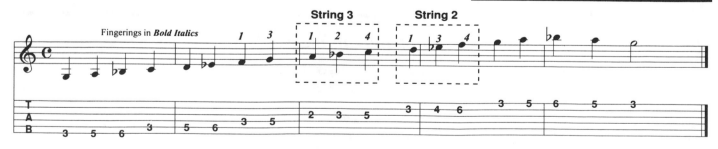

Fingerings in *Bold Italics*

String 3

String 2

G MAJOR SCALE:							
G A B C D E F# G							
1 2 3 4 5 6 7 1							

G Natural Minor

G	A	Bb	C	D	Eb	F	G
ROOT	SECOND	FLAT 3rd	FOURTH	FIFTH	FLAT 6th	FLAT 7th	

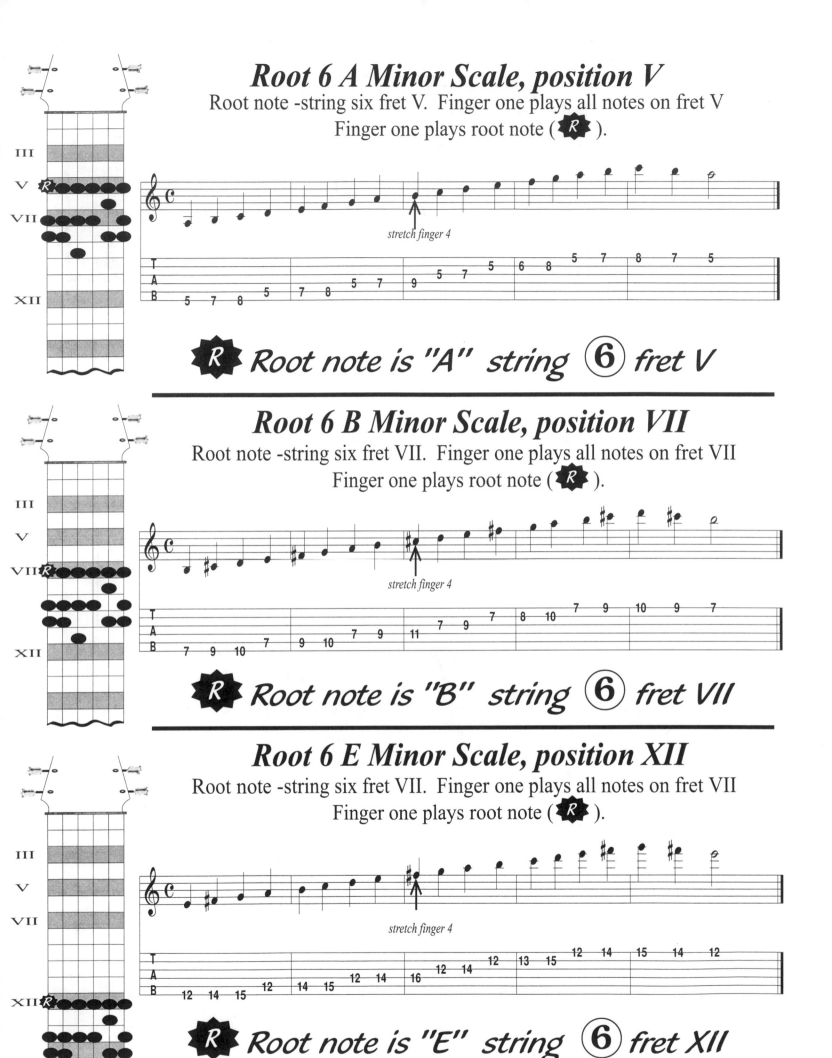

Root 6 A Minor Scale, position V

Root note -string six fret V. Finger one plays all notes on fret V
Finger one plays root note (R).

stretch finger 4

R Root note is "A" string ⑥ fret V

Root 6 B Minor Scale, position VII

Root note -string six fret VII. Finger one plays all notes on fret VII
Finger one plays root note (R).

stretch finger 4

R Root note is "B" string ⑥ fret VII

Root 6 E Minor Scale, position XII

Root note -string six fret VII. Finger one plays all notes on fret VII
Finger one plays root note (R).

stretch finger 4

R Root note is "E" string ⑥ fret XII

65

Root 5 Natural minor Scales

C Natural Minor, Position III

The *natural minor* is also known as the *'pure'* or *'Aeolian minor'* scale. Use the C minor scale against a Cmi chord or simple rock type progression which cadences to a C mi chord. Such as ➤

C MAJOR SCALE:	C Natural Minor						
CDEFGABC	C	D	Eb	F	G	Ab	Bb C
1234567 1	ROOT	SECOND	FLAT 3rd	FOURTH	FIFTH	FLAT 6th	FLAT 7th

C Natural Minor, Extended

The illustration below shows all notes in the third position which belong to the C Natural minor scale.

66

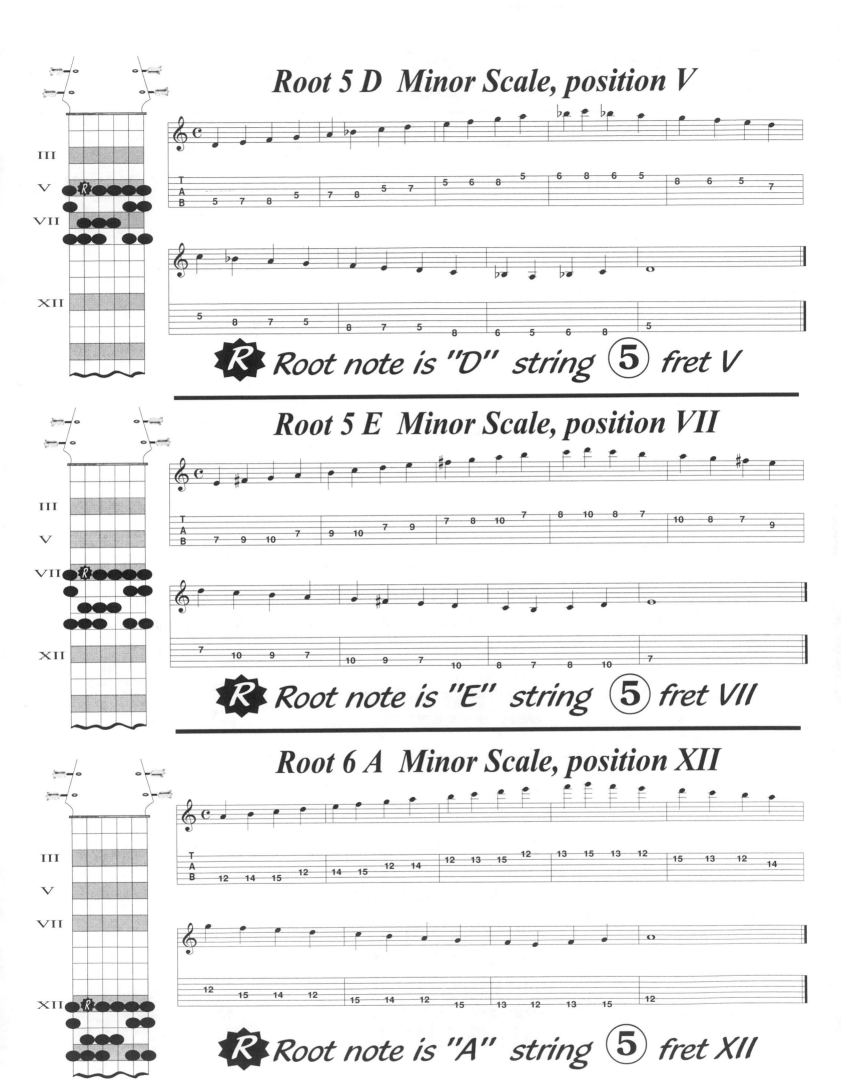

Root 5 D Minor Scale, position V

R Root note is "D" string ⑤ fret V

Root 5 E Minor Scale, position VII

R Root note is "E" string ⑤ fret VII

Root 6 A Minor Scale, position XII

R Root note is "A" string ⑤ fret XII

Applying The 5 Essential Root Six Scales

In pop, rock, jazz and blues guitar playing the most common scale sounds are
MINOR PENTATONIC ✎ **BLUES** ✎ **MAJOR PENTATONIC** ✎ **MAJOR** ✎ **MINOR**

In all of music there are three basic chord sounds:
MAJOR ✎ **MINOR** ✎ **DOMINANT SEVEN**

Its possible to play hot solos based on one scale, use the chart below to determine which scale will fit with a given chord.

ROOT 6 MINOR PENTATONIC

Creates the funky, rockin', cool, 'bad' sound most often heard in hot rock guitar playing. Number one scale in lead guitar playing.

G Ma	G mi	G 7 dominant

BLEND WITH ➡

BLUES SCALE

Bluesy, soulful, funky and down home. The sweet smooth sister of the minor pentatonic. Used by all big time rock and blues guitarists.

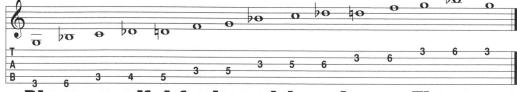

G Ma	G mi	G 7 dominant

BLEND WITH ➡

ROOT 6 MAJOR PENTATONIC

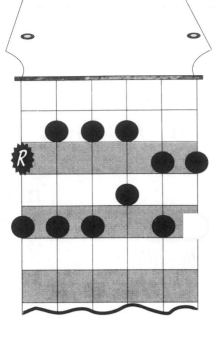

Sweet, melodic and pretty sounds are made by the Major pentatonic. Tuneful, beautiful, soulful and powerful. A favorite of the Allman Bros. Band.

G Ma   G 7 dominant

 BLEND WITH

ROOT 6 MAJOR

The foundation of music theory and the most used and played scale in all of music. The Major scale is bright, happy and melodic.

G Ma

 BLEND WITH

ROOT 6 MINOR

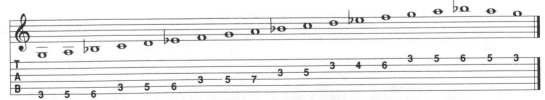

Dark, melodic and tuneful. The minor scale often sounds sad and mysterious. Favored by Carlos Santana.

G mi

BLEND WITH

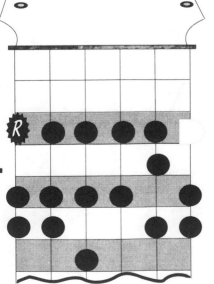

Applying The 5 Essential Root Five Scales

Most rock, pop and blues songs *(or solo sections of songs)* have a general overall sound to them; either

MAJOR ✒ **MINOR** ✒ **DOMINANT**

This is called their *key* or *tonality*.

Its possible to play hot solos based on one scale, use the chart below to determine which scale will fit with a given chord.

BEGIN TO IMPROVISE BY BASING YOUR ENTIRE SOLO ON ONE GENERAL OVERALL SCALE SOUND.

ROOT 5 MINOR PENTATONIC

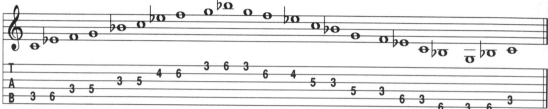

The main ingredient in rock and blues soloing is hallmark in the playing of Jimi Hendrix, Jimmy Page, Eric Clapton and Stevie Ray Vaughn.

BLEND WITH

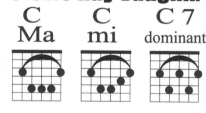

C Ma   C mi   C 7 dominant

BLUES SCALE

slide finger one

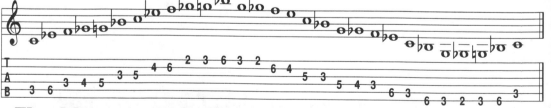

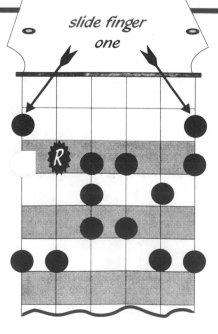

The blues scale is often heard from B.B. King, Buddy Guy, Eric Clapton and the inimitable Johnny Winter.

BLEND WITH

C Ma   C mi   C 7 dominant

70

ROOT 5 MAJOR PENTATONIC

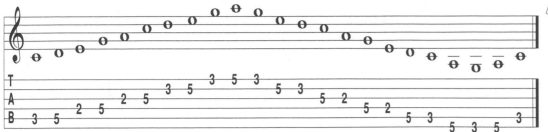

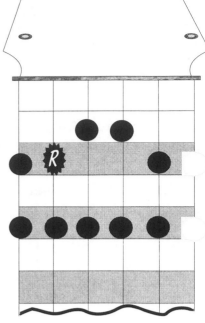

The melodious and tuneful major pentatonic scale is favored by Robin Ford and Dickey Betts.

C Ma   C 7 dominant

 BLEND WITH

ROOT 5 MAJOR

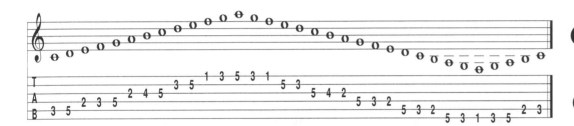

stretch finger one

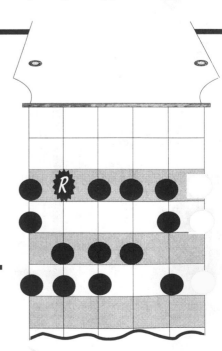

DO, RE, MI, FA, SOL, LA, TI, DO. The most important scale in all of music.

C Ma

 BLEND WITH

ROOT 5 MINOR

Dark, melodic and tuneful. The minor scale often sounds sad and mysterious.

C mi

 BLEND WITH

Five Position Thinking: Major Scales

The standard line of thinking among professional and serious guitarists is called **Position Playing** or **Five Position Thinking.** For every musical scale *(and chord)* there are five successive connected patterns on the guitar.

The large diagram below illustrates this concept of the five positions by highlighting every note which is a member of the C Major scale. I call this the **C Major Scale Super Pattern.**

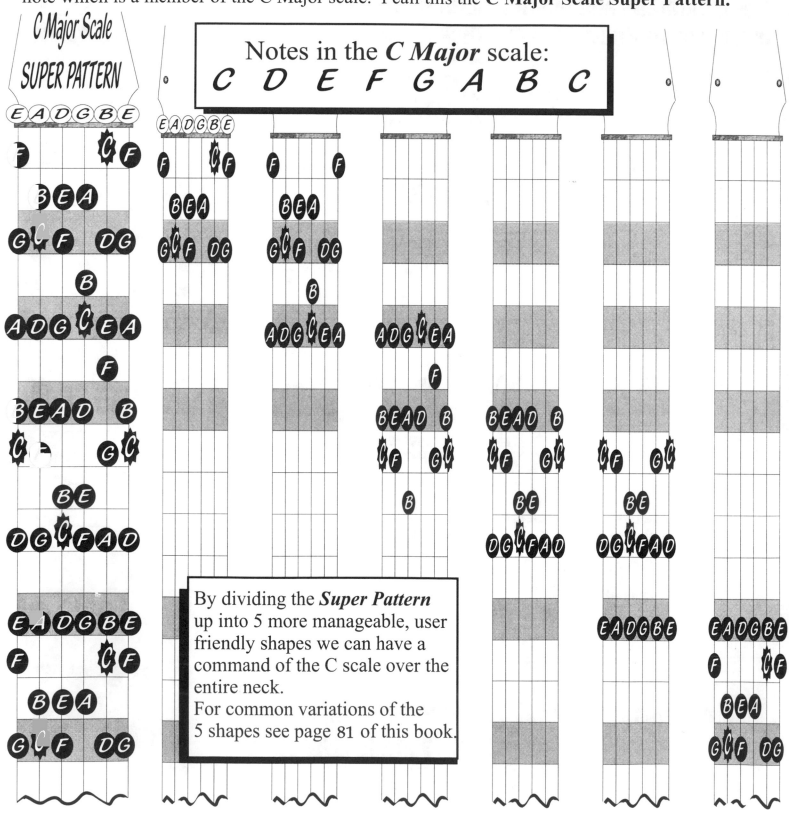

C Major Scale SUPER PATTERN

Notes in the *C Major* scale:
C D E F G A B C

By dividing the *Super Pattern* up into 5 more manageable, user friendly shapes we can have a command of the C scale over the entire neck.
For common variations of the 5 shapes see page 81 of this book.

Five Position Thinking: Chords

Below is a diagram of the **C Major Chord Super Patter**n and the five basic chord shapes of a C Major Chord. Memorizing Chord shapes in terms of connecting patterns is a big part of what learning the guitar is all about.

Practice playing the 5 basic Major chord shapes in all 12 keys.*

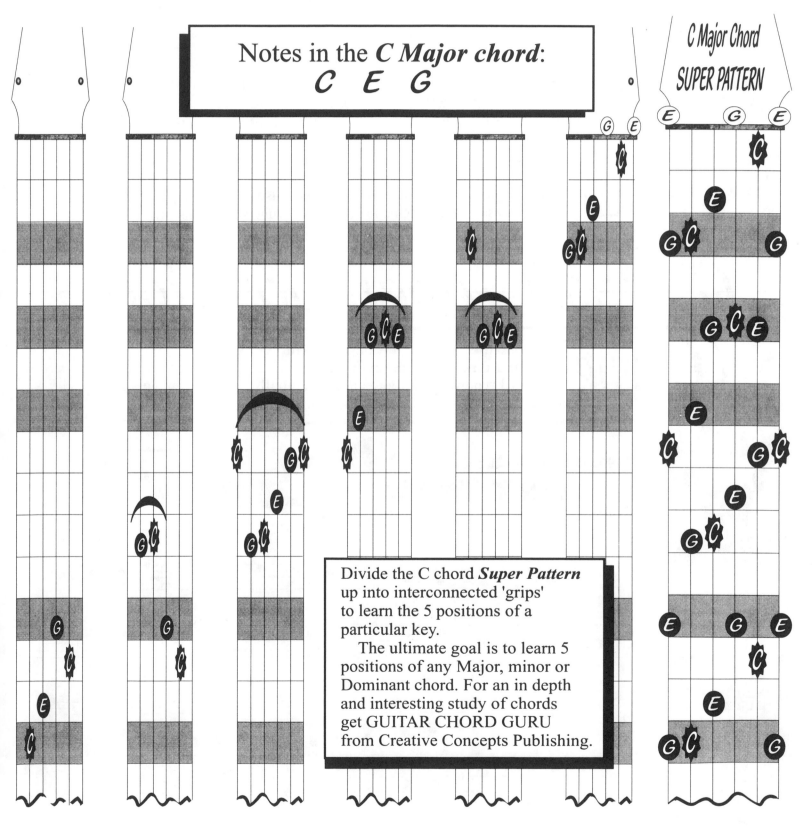

Notes in the *C Major chord*:
C E G

C Major Chord
SUPER PATTERN

Divide the C chord *Super Pattern* up into interconnected 'grips' to learn the 5 positions of a particular key.

The ultimate goal is to learn 5 positions of any Major, minor or Dominant chord. For an in depth and interesting study of chords get GUITAR CHORD GURU from Creative Concepts Publishing.

The Linking System

To quickly learn 5 positions of any scale, center your thinking around 5 plain old chords in the open position:

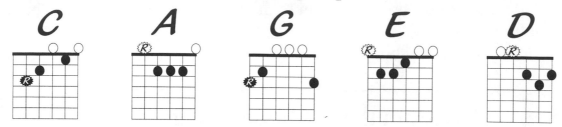

C   A   G   E   D

Each one of the 5 chords in this system is thought of as movable chord. By moving these chords up the neck, its possible to play each one of the 5 chords with a root note of **"C"**. For example, when every note in a basic **A Major** chord is raised in pitch by three frets *(see top of pg. 75)* the resulting chord is **C Major,** which has a shape and appearance just like the plain old **A Major chord** we started out with except for the fact that's its now on the third fret. Thinking of 5 open string chords (C, A, G, E, D) in this manner is called the **CAGED SYSTEM**.

    If its possible to play 5 different versions of a **C Major chord,** then its also possible to play 5 different versions of a **C Major scale.** I've found that associating each one of the 5 "C" chords with its own individual fingering for a **C Major scale** is a powerful learning tool. I call this **THE LINKING SYSTEM.**

C Major -open position

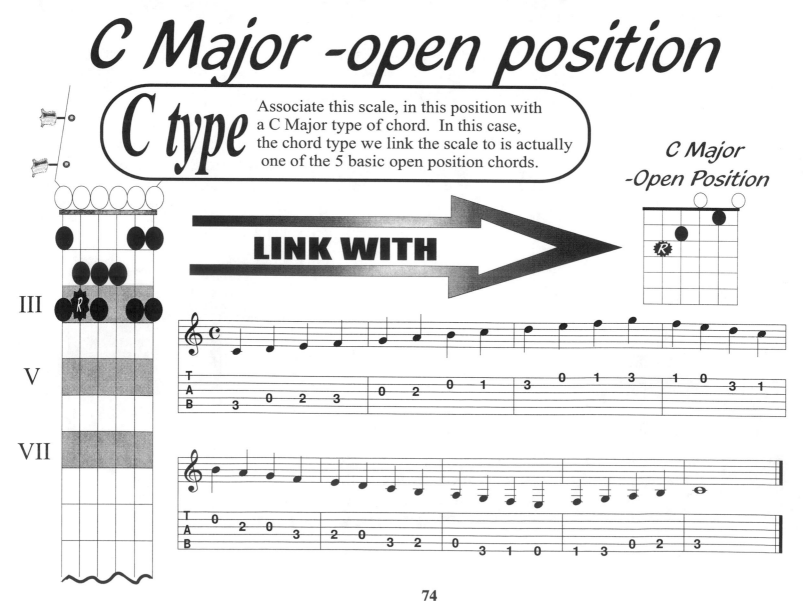

C type — Associate this scale, in this position with a C Major type of chord. In this case, the chord type we link the scale to is actually one of the 5 basic open position chords.

C Major -Open Position

LINK WITH

C Major -second position

A type

Associate the C major scale, in position II with an **A Major type of chord**: when a basic open string A chord is moved up the neck *(higher in pitch)* 3 frets, the result is a C Major, position III.

LINK WITH

C Major -Third Position

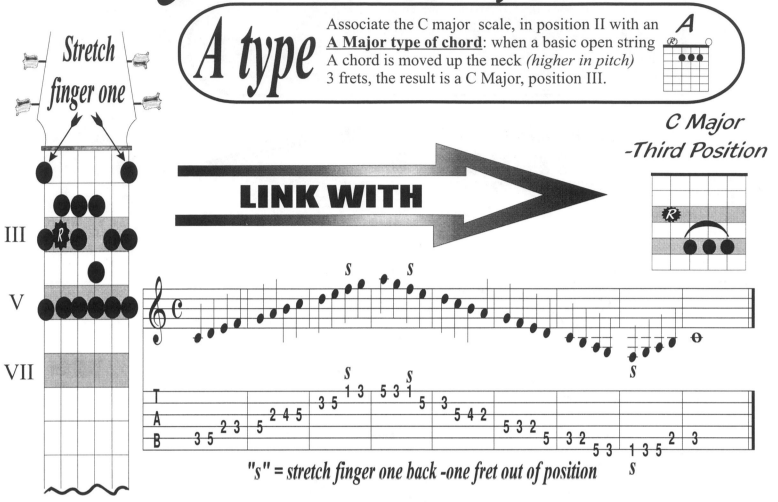

Stretch finger one

III
V
VII

s = *stretch finger one back -one fret out of position*

Optional C Major scale -Positions II & III

LINK WITH

C Major -Third Position

This very common and comfortable option for a C scale involves shifting positions on string 2, thereby eliminating the need to stretch finger one back to fret I for the F note *(see also, pg. 41)*.

Although awkward at first, I recommend you learn to use the "stretching" version of the C scale on the top of this page as your first line of thinking concerning the 5 scale shapes.

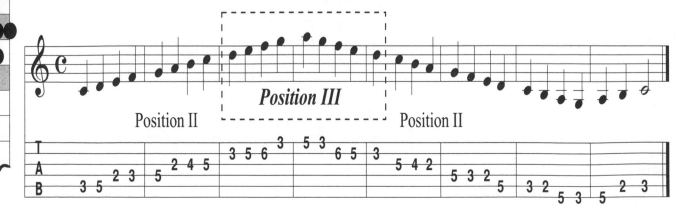

Position II   *Position III*   Position II

75

C Major -fifth position

G type

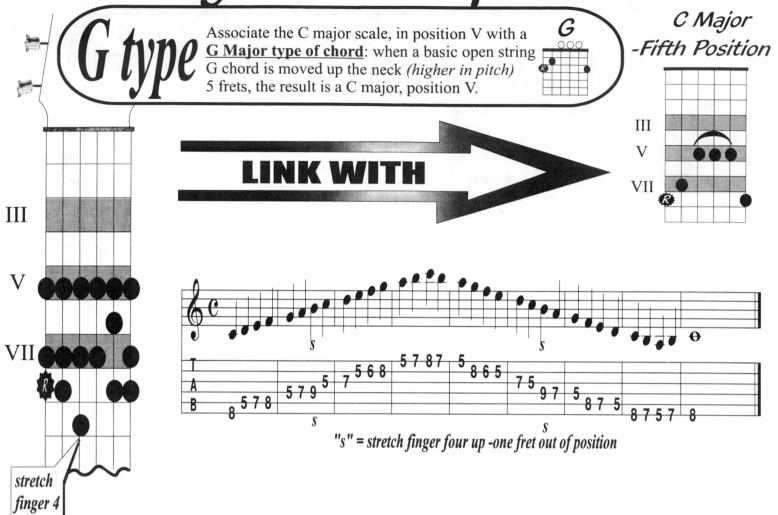

Associate the C major scale, in position V with a **G Major type of chord**: when a basic open string G chord is moved up the neck *(higher in pitch)* 5 frets, the result is a C major, position V.

LINK WITH

C Major -Fifth Position

III
V
VII

"s" = stretch finger four up -one fret out of position

stretch finger 4

Optional C Major scale -Positions IV & V

LINK WITH

C Major -Fifth Position

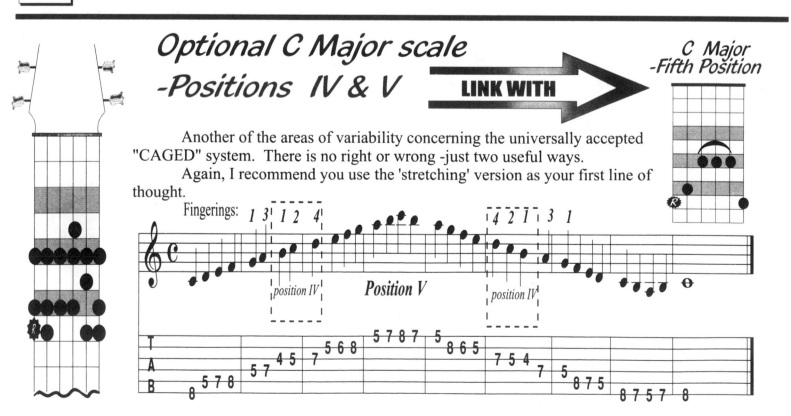

Another of the areas of variability concerning the universally accepted "CAGED" system. There is no right or wrong -just two useful ways.

Again, I recommend you use the 'stretching' version as your first line of thought.

Fingerings: 1 3 | 1 2 4   4 2 1 | 3 1

position IV   **Position V**   position IV

76

C Major -seventh position

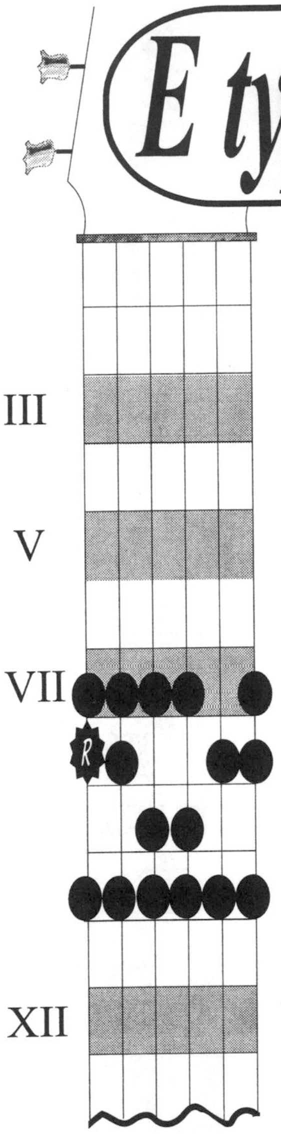

C Major -Eighth Position

E type. Associate the C major scale, in position VII with an *E* **E Major type of chord**: when a basic open string G chord is moved up the neck *(higher in pitch)* 8 frets, the result is a C Major, position VIII.

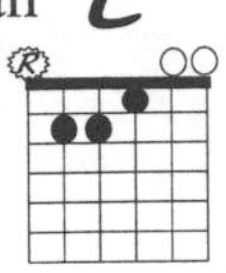

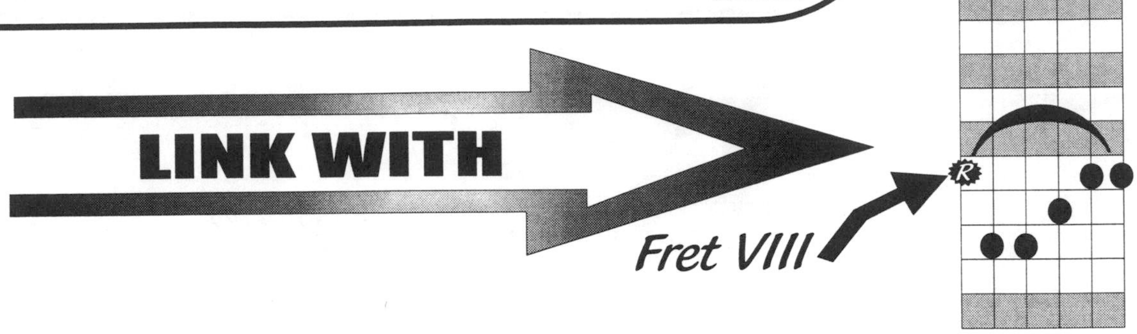

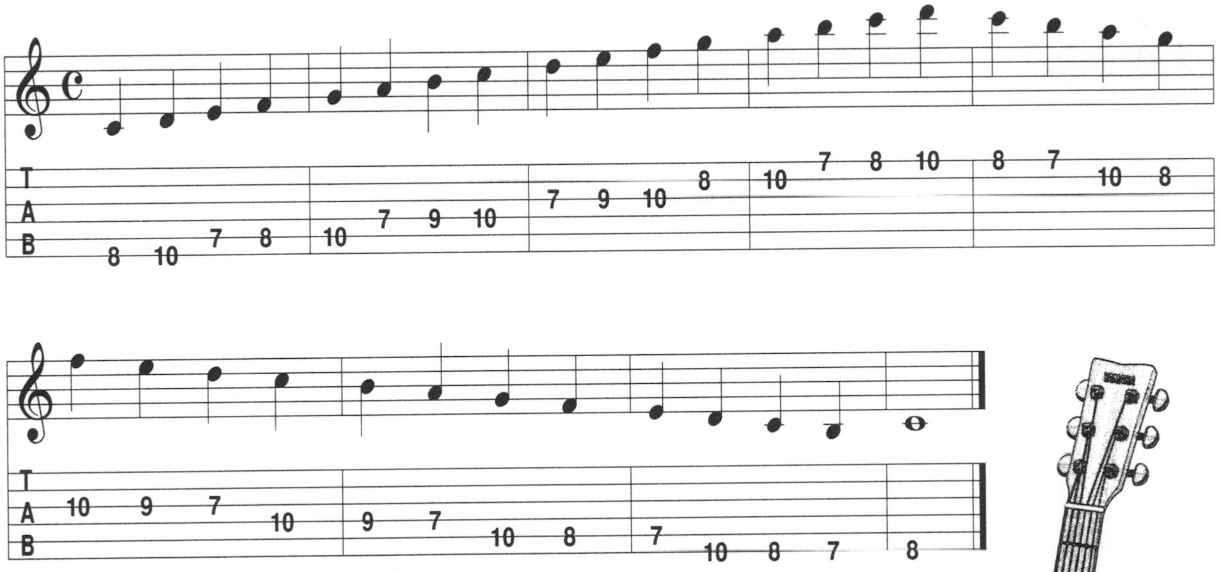

LINK WITH

Fret VIII

III

V

VII

XII

The most widely known and used form of a Major scale on the guitar *(see pg. 38)* is illustrated above in the key of C Major.

There can be no disagreement on this form of a Major scale being the one to associate with a garden variety root 6 barre chord as I have done above.

The best way to go about a study of the guitar is to check out all the ideas and theories you can by building a huge library of books and taking lessons with qualified, experienced instructors.

The ideas that work best for you will surely present themselves as a by-product of hard work.

C Major -ninth position

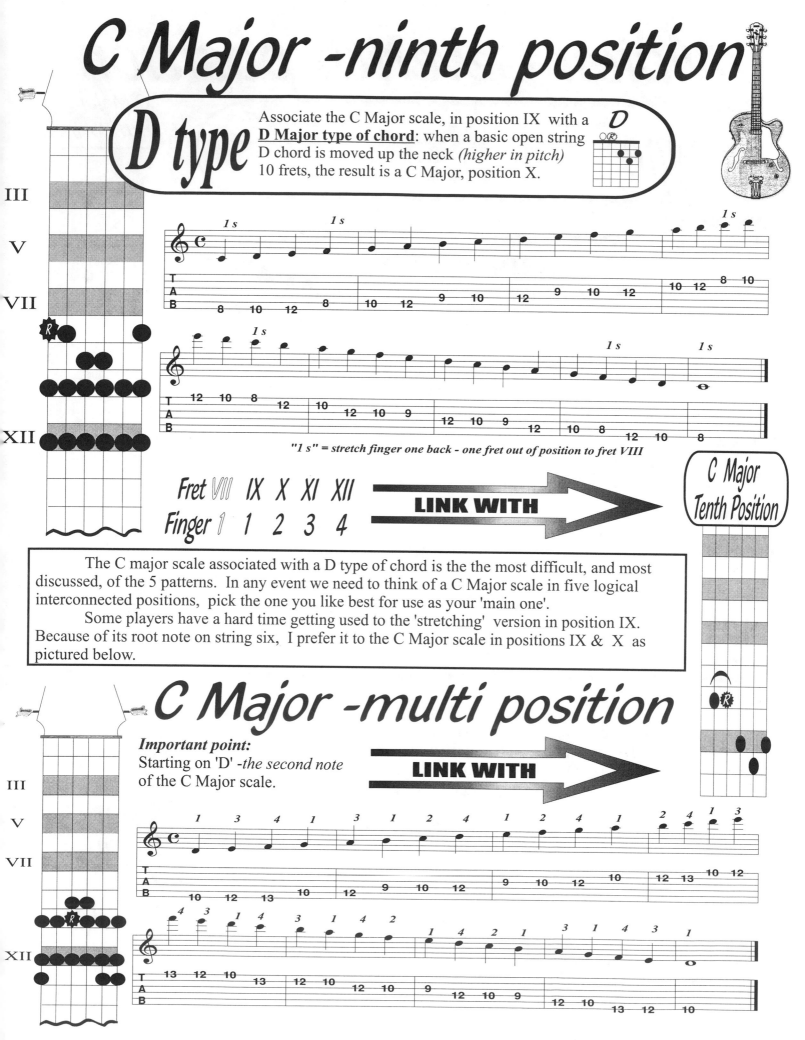

D type

Associate the C Major scale, in position IX with a **D Major type of chord**: when a basic open string D chord is moved up the neck *(higher in pitch)* 10 frets, the result is a C Major, position X.

"1 s" = stretch finger one back - one fret out of position to fret VIII

Fret VII IX X XI XII
Finger 1 1 2 3 4

LINK WITH ➡

C Major Tenth Position

The C major scale associated with a D type of chord is the the most difficult, and most discussed, of the 5 patterns. In any event we need to think of a C Major scale in five logical interconnected positions, pick the one you like best for use as your 'main one'.

Some players have a hard time getting used to the 'stretching' version in position IX. Because of its root note on string six, I prefer it to the C Major scale in positions IX & X as pictured below.

C Major -multi position

Important point:
Starting on 'D' -*the second note* of the C Major scale.

LINK WITH ➡

78

C Major -twelfth position

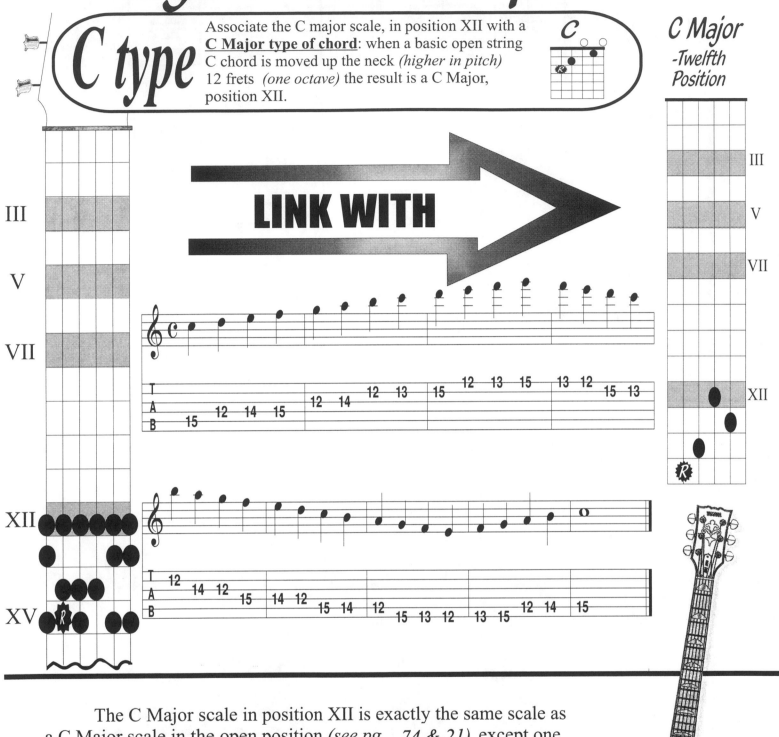

C type — Associate the C major scale, in position XII with a **C Major type of chord**: when a basic open string C chord is moved up the neck *(higher in pitch)* 12 frets *(one octave)* the result is a C Major, position XII.

C Major -Twelfth Position

LINK WITH

The C Major scale in position XII is exactly the same scale as a C Major scale in the open position *(see pg. 74 & 21)* except one octave higher. Notes an octave above the open string notes appear on fret XII. The scale fingerings have now come full circle and begin to repeat themselves in the same order. This is the logic and beauty of 5 position thinking, learn it and use it well: you'll be in some very good company.

As with the 'E type' of scale illustrated on page 77, there can be no disagreement on this form of a C Major scale being the most logical and usable one to play in position XII.

The 5 basic shapes of a C Major chord.

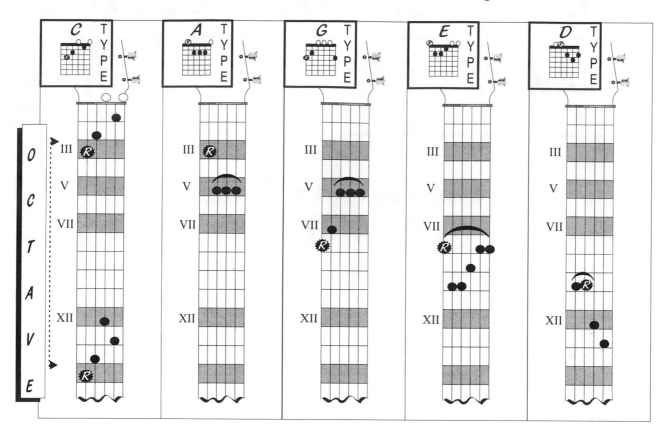

The 5 basic shapes of a C Major scale.

's' -means stretch finger 1 or 4 out of position

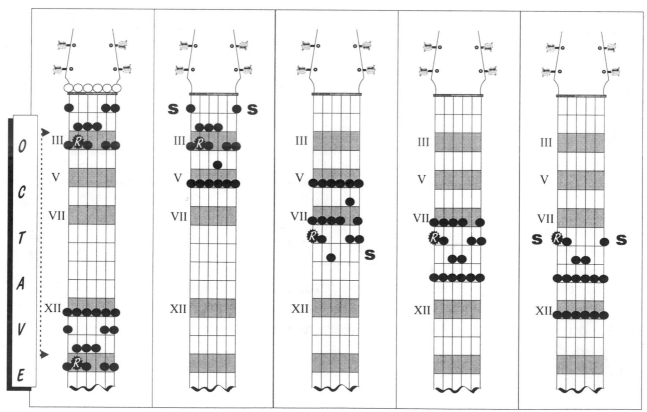

C Major: C D E F G A B C

Key Signature:

MAJOR KEYS

 C Type

As you learn the 5 basic shapes of every Major Chord * associate a Major scale pattern with each chord shape. The root note of the chord will also be the root note of the scale in your new system of thinking. Every serious guitar student must master this concept.

 A Type

Every scale shape is not as clear and logical as the **C type.** If the **A type** of scale is to be played strictly in position, you must temporarily stretch the first finger back one fret out of position.

 G Type

If the **G type** of Major scale is to be played strictly in position, you must temporarily stretch the fourth finger up one fret out of position. Use the sliding, multi position version offered as a *'speed'* option.

 E Type

The **E type** of Major scale is to be played strictly in position. This is one of those clear, logical universally agreed upon principles of guitar playing. This is probably the most used form of a Major scale.

 D Type

The **D type** is the most discussed Major scale. If you don't like to stretch, then you must slide. I learned to use the stretching version of this scale as part of my training with the great Bill Leavitt.

Voicings based upon
"GUITAR CHORD GURU -The Chord Book"
by Creative Concepts.

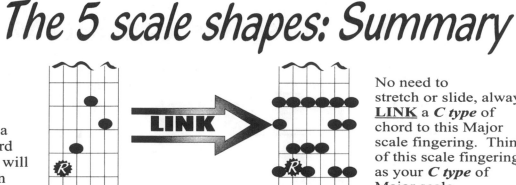

 **LINK**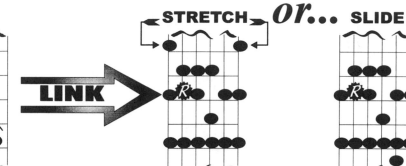

No need to stretch or slide, always **LINK** a **C type** of chord to this Major scale fingering. Think of this scale fingering as your **C type** of Major scale.

STRETCH *or...* **SLIDE**

 **LINK**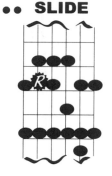

STRETCH ➤ *or...* **SLIDE**

 **LINK**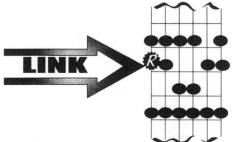

No need to stretch or slide, always **LINK** an **E type** of chord to this Major scale fingering. Think of this scale fingering as your **E type** of major scale.

STRETCH *or...* **SHIFT**

 **LINK**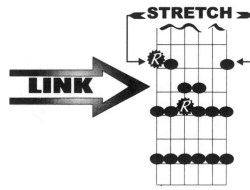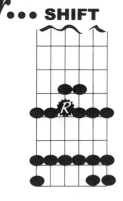

The 5 basic shapes of a G Major chord.

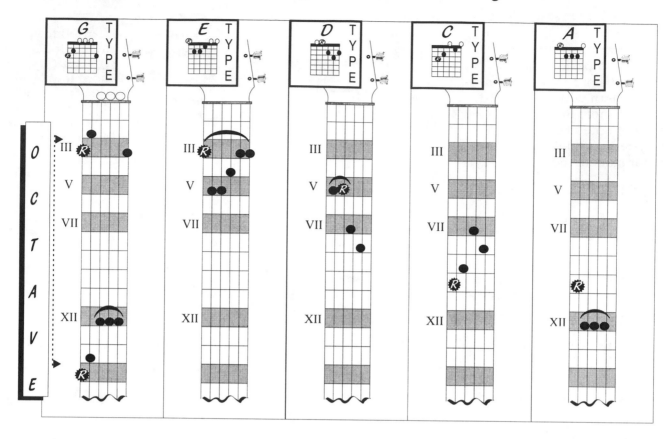

The 5 basic shapes of a G Major scale.

's' -means stretch finger 1 or 4 out of position

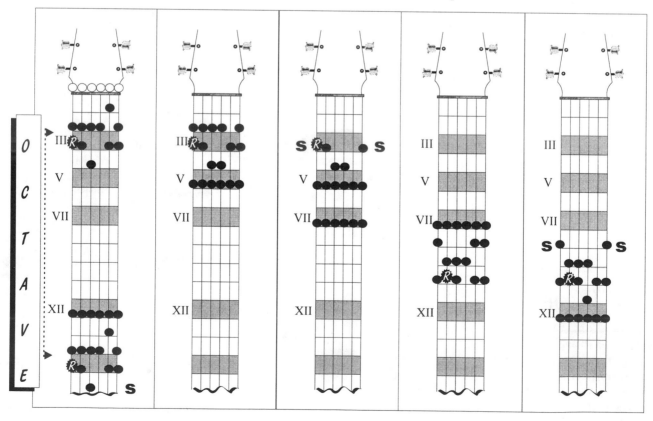

G Major: G A B C D E F#G

82

Key Signature:

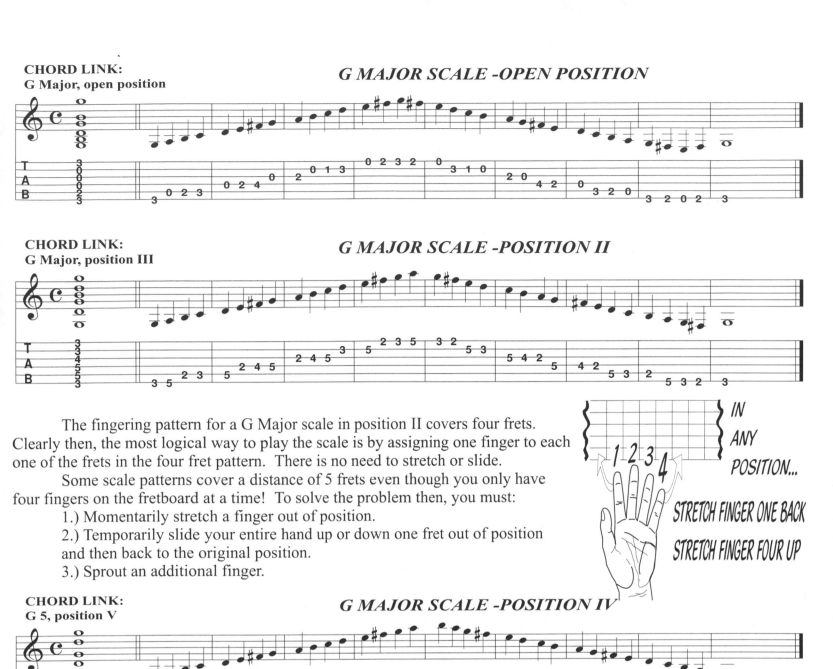

CHORD LINK:
G Major, open position

G MAJOR SCALE -OPEN POSITION

CHORD LINK:
G Major, position III

G MAJOR SCALE -POSITION II

The fingering pattern for a G Major scale in position II covers four frets. Clearly then, the most logical way to play the scale is by assigning one finger to each one of the frets in the four fret pattern. There is no need to stretch or slide.

Some scale patterns cover a distance of 5 frets even though you only have four fingers on the fretboard at a time! To solve the problem then, you must:

1.) Momentarily stretch a finger out of position.

2.) Temporarily slide your entire hand up or down one fret out of position and then back to the original position.

3.) Sprout an additional finger.

IN ANY POSITION...

STRETCH FINGER ONE BACK
STRETCH FINGER FOUR UP

CHORD LINK:
G 5, position V

G MAJOR SCALE -POSITION IV

CHORD LINK:
G Major, position VII

G MAJOR SCALE -POSITION VII

CHORD LINK:
G Major, position X

G MAJOR SCALE -POSITION IX

The 5 basic shapes of a D Major chord.

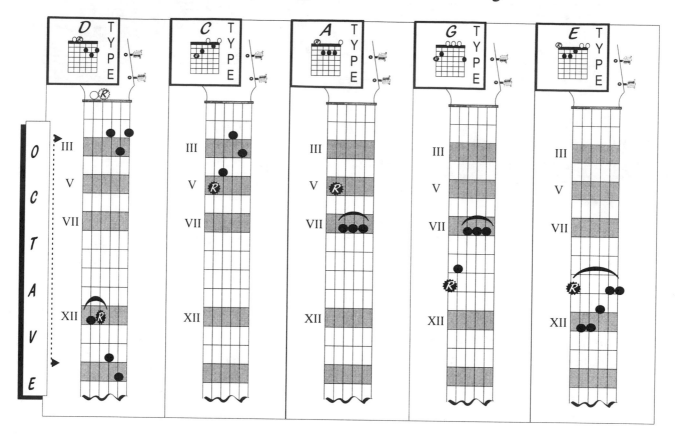

The 5 basic shapes of a D Major scale.*

D Major: D E F# G A B C# D   **Key Signature:**

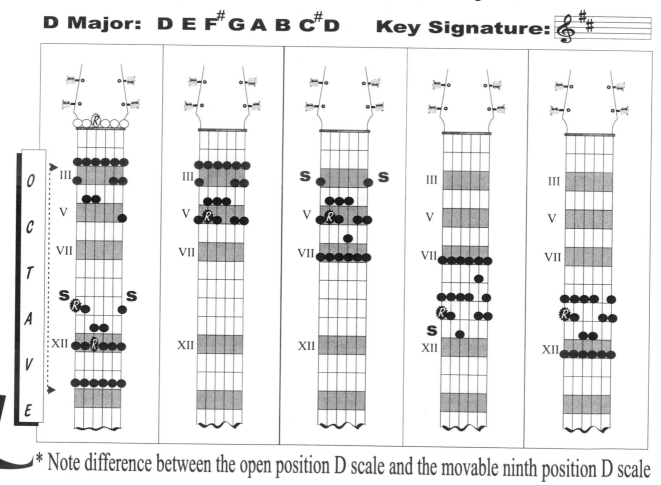

* Note difference between the open position D scale and the movable ninth position D scale

's' -means stretch finger 1 or 4 out of position

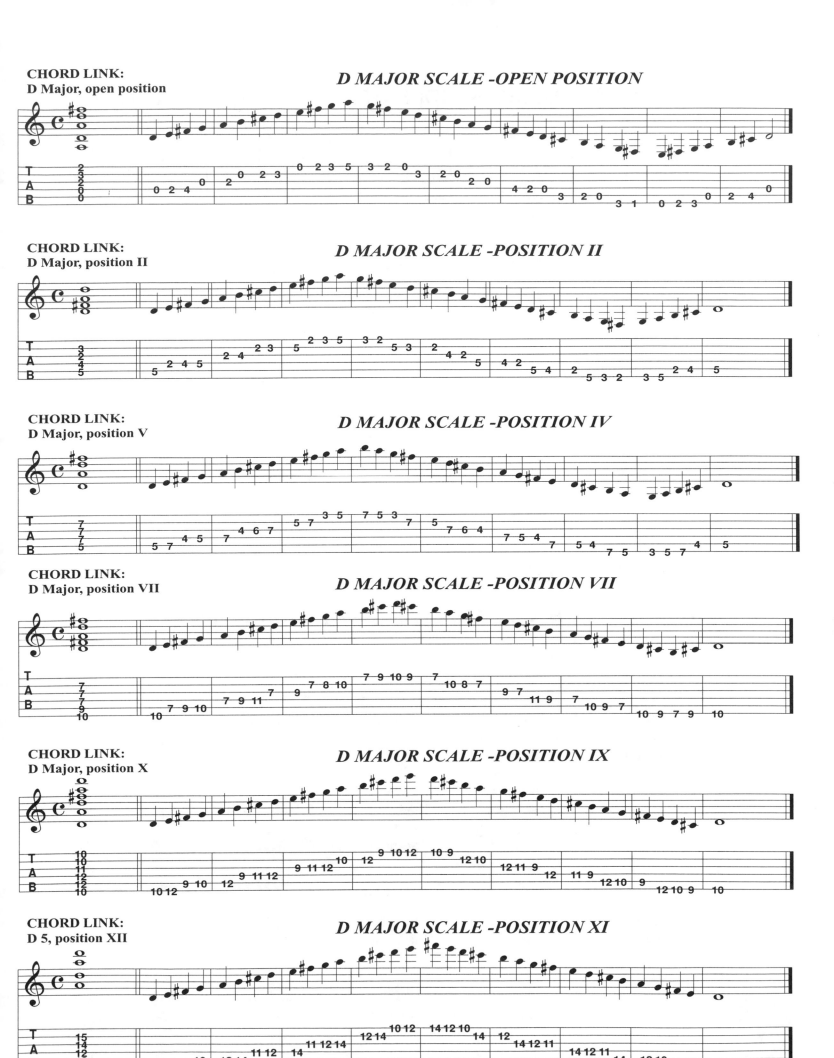

85

The 5 basic shapes of an A Major chord.

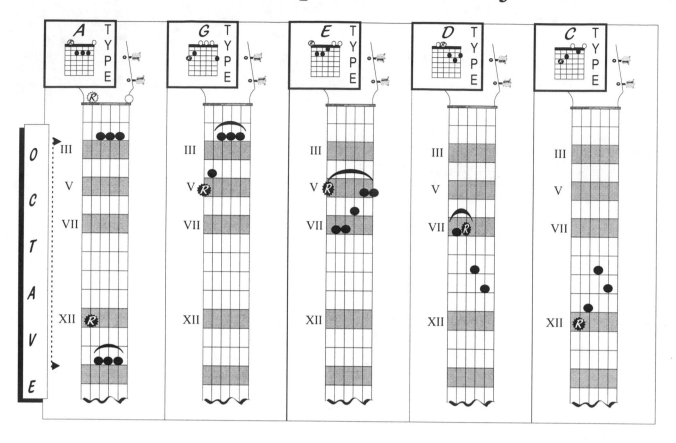

The 5 basic shapes of an A Major scale.*

A Major: A B C#D E F#G#A   Key Signature:

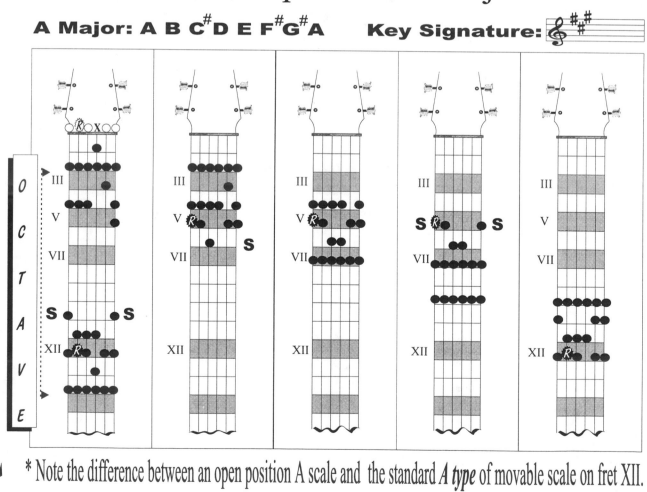

*Note the difference between an open position A scale and the standard *A type* of movable scale on fret XII.*

's' -means stretch finger 1 or 4 out of position

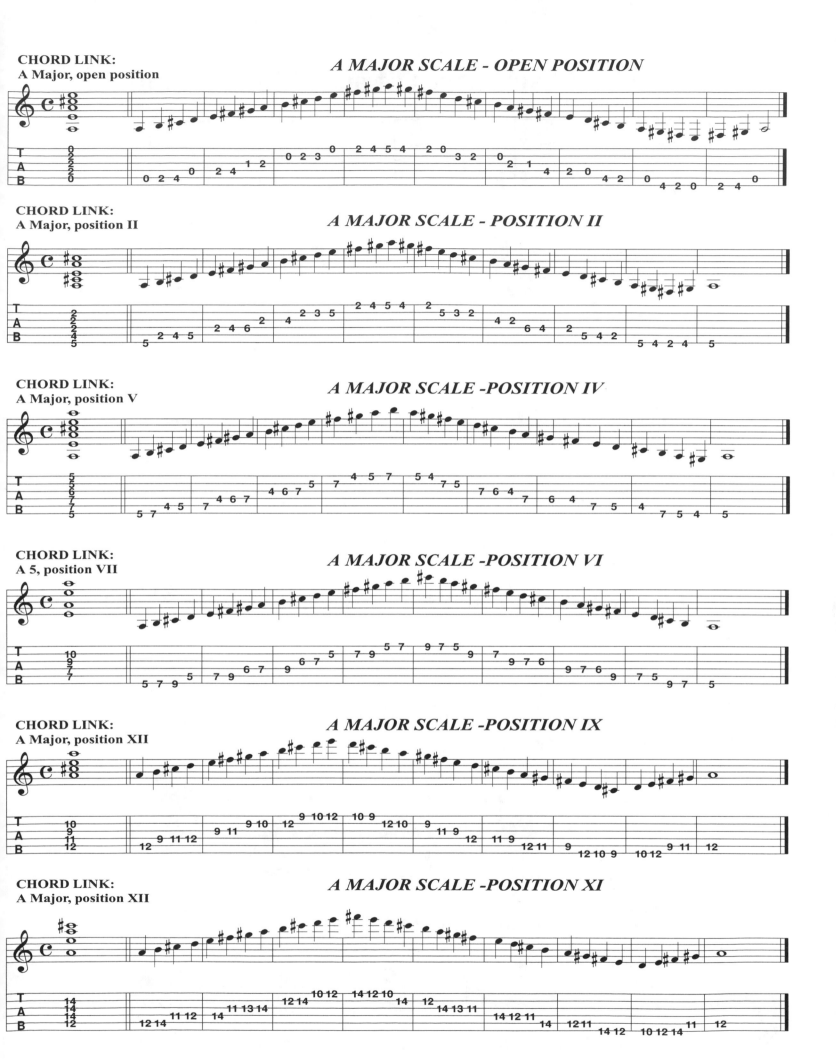

87

The 5 basic shapes of an E Major chord.

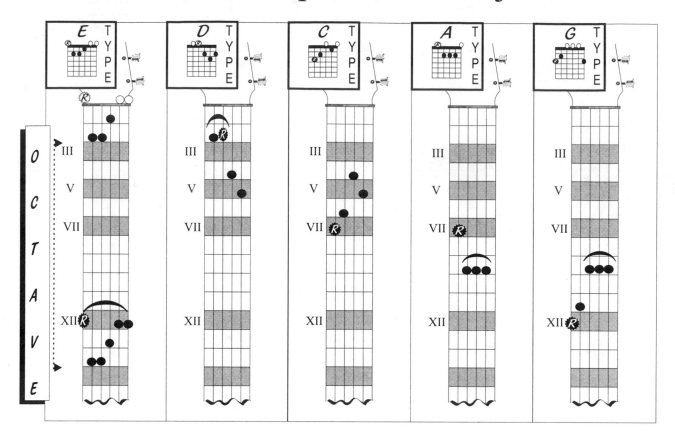

The 5 basic shapes of an E Major scale.*

E Major: E F#G#A B C#D#E   **Key Signature:**

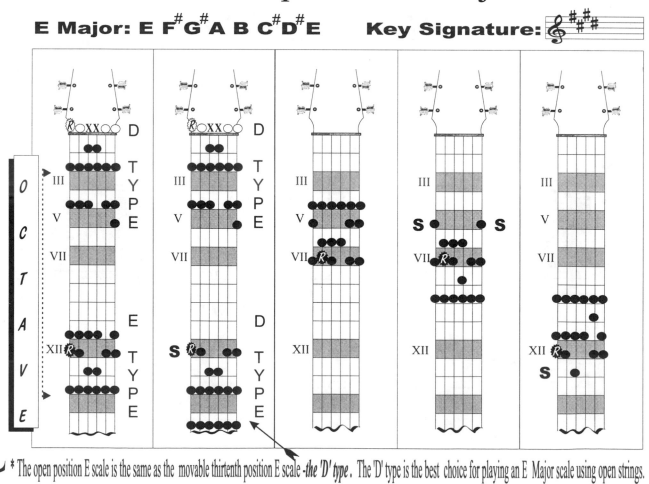

* The open position E scale is the same as the movable thirtenth position E scale -the 'D' type. The 'D' type is the best choice for playing an E Major scale using open strings.

's' -means stretch finger 1 or 4 out of position

CHORD LINK:
E Major, Open position

E MAJOR SCALE -OPEN POSITION

CHORD LINK:
E Major, position II

E MAJOR SCALE -OPEN POSITION

CHORD LINK:
E Major, position IV

E MAJOR SCALE -POSITION IV

CHORD LINK:
E Major, position VII

E MAJOR SCALE -POSITION VI

CHORD LINK:
E Major, position IX

E MAJOR SCALE - POSITION IX

CHORD LINK:
E Major, position XII

E MAJOR SCALE -POSITION XI

The 5 basic shapes of a B Major chord.

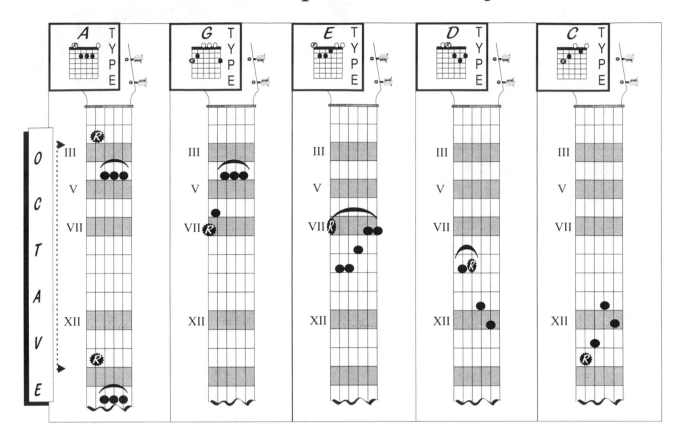

The 5 basic shapes of a B Major scale.

's' -means stretch finger 1 or 4 out of position

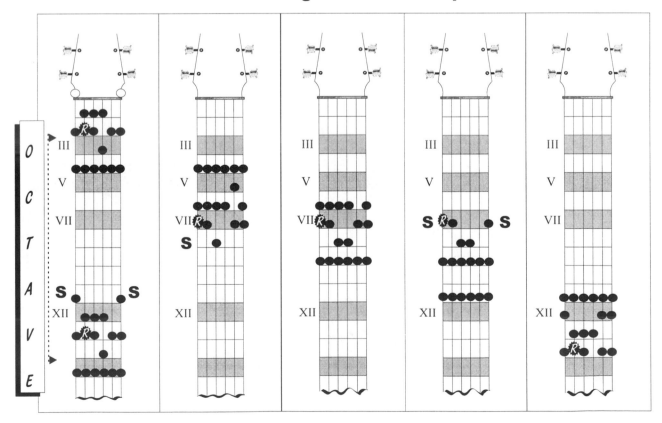

B Major: B C[#]D[#] E F[#]G[#]A[#] B

Key Signature:

CHORD LINK:
B Major, position II

B MAJOR SCALE -OPEN POSITION

CHORD LINK:
B Major, position IV

B MAJOR SCALE - POSITION IV

CHORD LINK:
B Major, position VII

B MAJOR SCALE -POSITION VII

CHORD LINK:
B 5, position IX

B MAJOR SCALE -POSITION VIII

CHORD LINK:
B Major, position XI

B MAJOR SCALE -POSITION XI

CHORD LINK:
B Major, position II

B MAJOR SCALE -POSITION I

8va means play one octave higher than written.

The 5 basic shapes of an F Major chord.

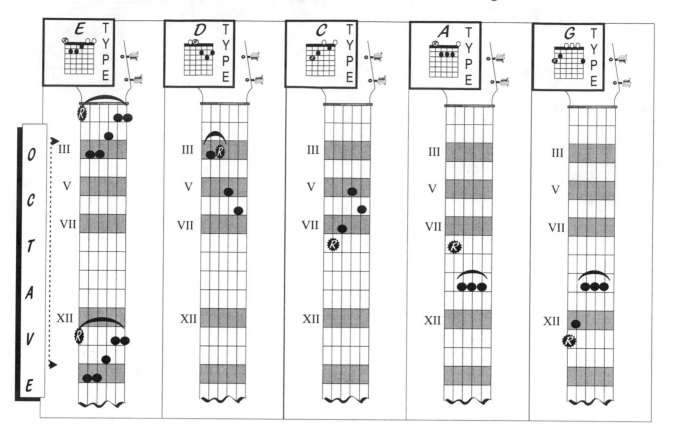

The 5 basic shapes of an F Major scale.

's' -means stretch finger 1 or 4 out of position

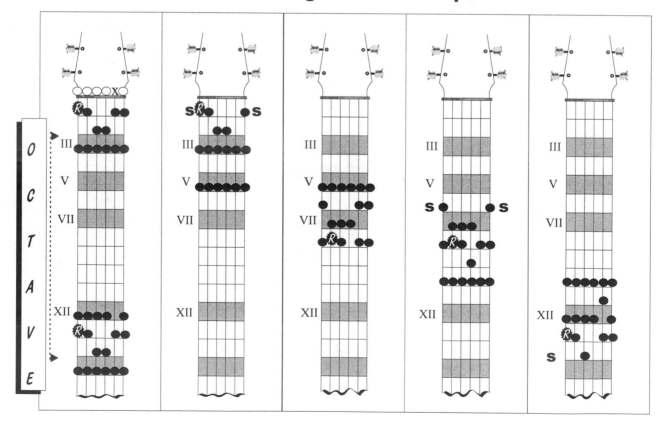

F Major: F G A B♭ C D E F

Key Signature: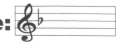

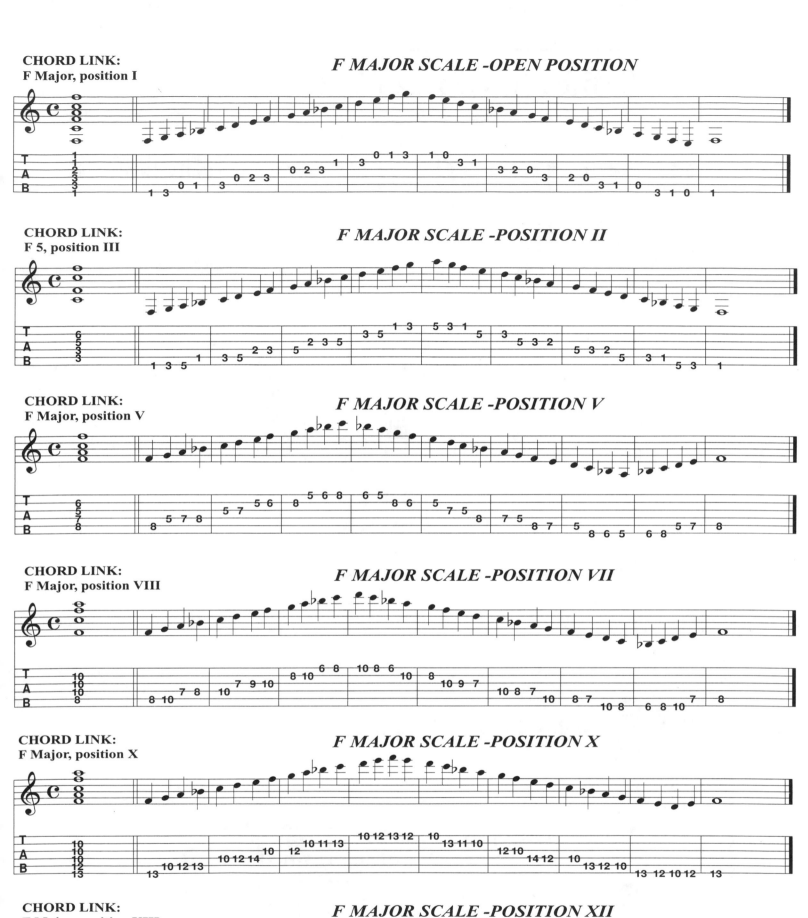

93

Concept of the C Major Scale

W W 1/2 W W W 1/2

Whole **W**hole 1/2 **W**hole **W**hole **W**hole 1/2

The theory of the Major Scale is expressed by a formula consisting of half steps and whole steps.

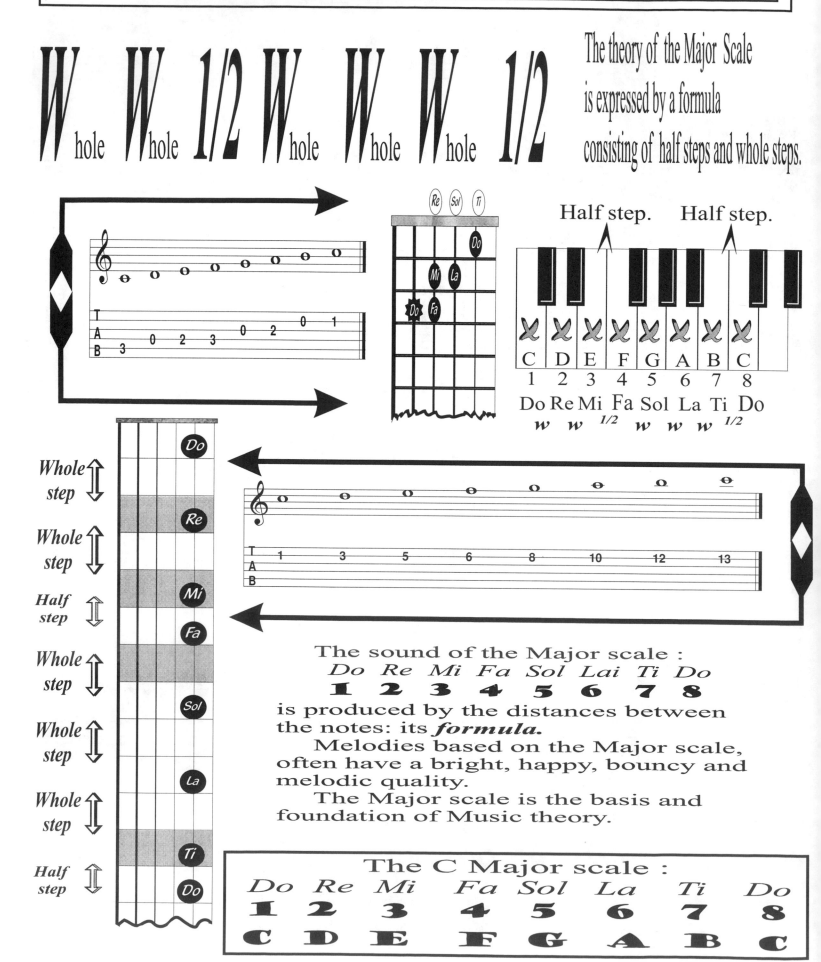

The sound of the Major scale :
Do Re Mi Fa Sol Lai Ti Do
1 2 3 4 5 6 7 8
is produced by the distances between the notes: its *formula.*

Melodies based on the Major scale, often have a bright, happy, bouncy and melodic quality.

The Major scale is the basis and foundation of Music theory.

The C Major scale :

Do	Re	Mi	Fa	Sol	La	Ti	Do
1	2	3	4	5	6	7	8
C	D	E	F	G	A	B	C

Concept of the C minor Scale

The theory of the minor Scale is expressed by a new formula consisting of half steps and whole steps.

Half step.   Half step.

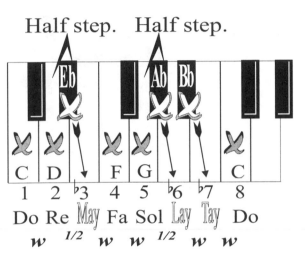

C D ♭3 F G ♭6 ♭7 C
1 2 3   4 5 6   7   8

Do Re May Fa Sol Lay Tay Do
w   1/2 w w 1/2 w w

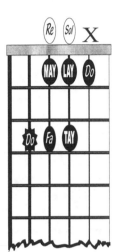

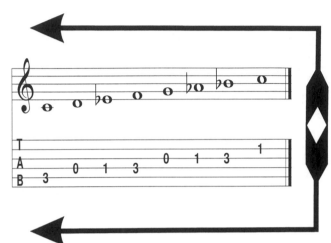

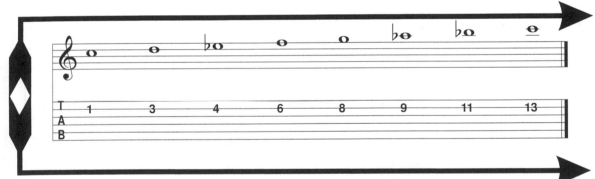

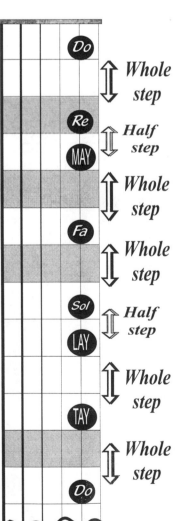

The sound of the minor scale :

Do Re May Fa Sol Lay Tay Do
1 2 ♭3 4 5 ♭6 ♭7 8

is produced by the distances between the notes: its *formula.*

Melodies based on the Minor scale, often have a dark, sad or mysterious quality.

When the C minor scale is compared to the C Major scale the minor scale is said to have a *flatted 3rd, 6th* and *7th.*

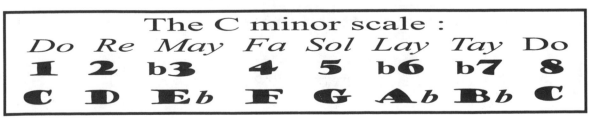

The C minor scale :

Do	Re	May	Fa	Sol	Lay	Tay	Do
1	**2**	**♭3**	**4**	**5**	**♭6**	**♭7**	**8**
C	**D**	**E♭**	**F**	**G**	**A♭**	**B♭**	**C**

Diatonic Melodies

1.) Play a C Major chord.

2.) Play a C Major scale.

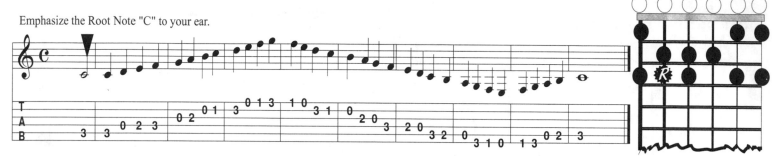

Emphasize the Root Note "C" to your ear.

3.) Learn the following diatonic melodies.

WHEN THE SAINTS GO MARCHING IN

POP GOES THE WEASEL

FRERE JACQUES

Minor scale Melodies

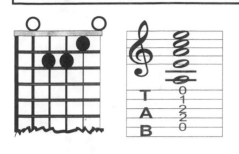 

1.) Play an A minor chord.

2.) Play an A minor scale.

Emphasize the Root Note "A" to your ear.

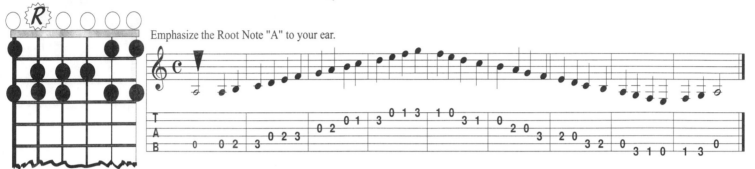

3.) Learn the following minor melodies.

SNAKE CHARMING TYPE OF LICK

FUNERAL MARCH

GREENSLEEVES

GOD REST YE MERRY GENTLEMEN

Minor scales in the Open Position

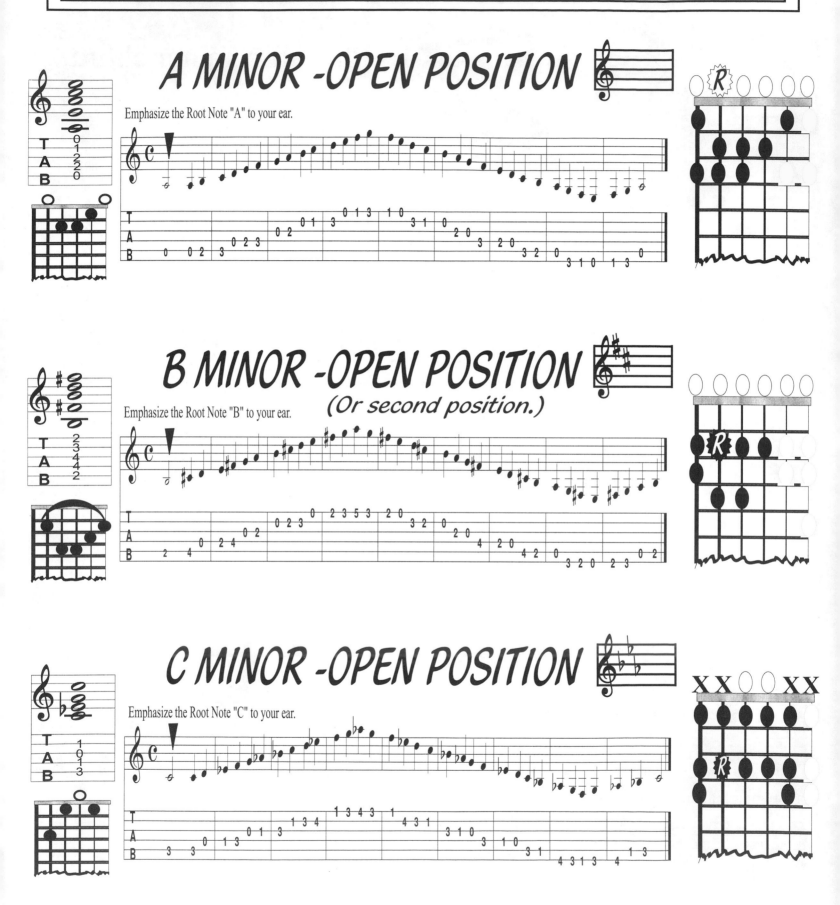

A MINOR -OPEN POSITION

Emphasize the Root Note "A" to your ear.

B MINOR -OPEN POSITION
(Or second position.)

Emphasize the Root Note "B" to your ear.

C MINOR -OPEN POSITION

Emphasize the Root Note "C" to your ear.

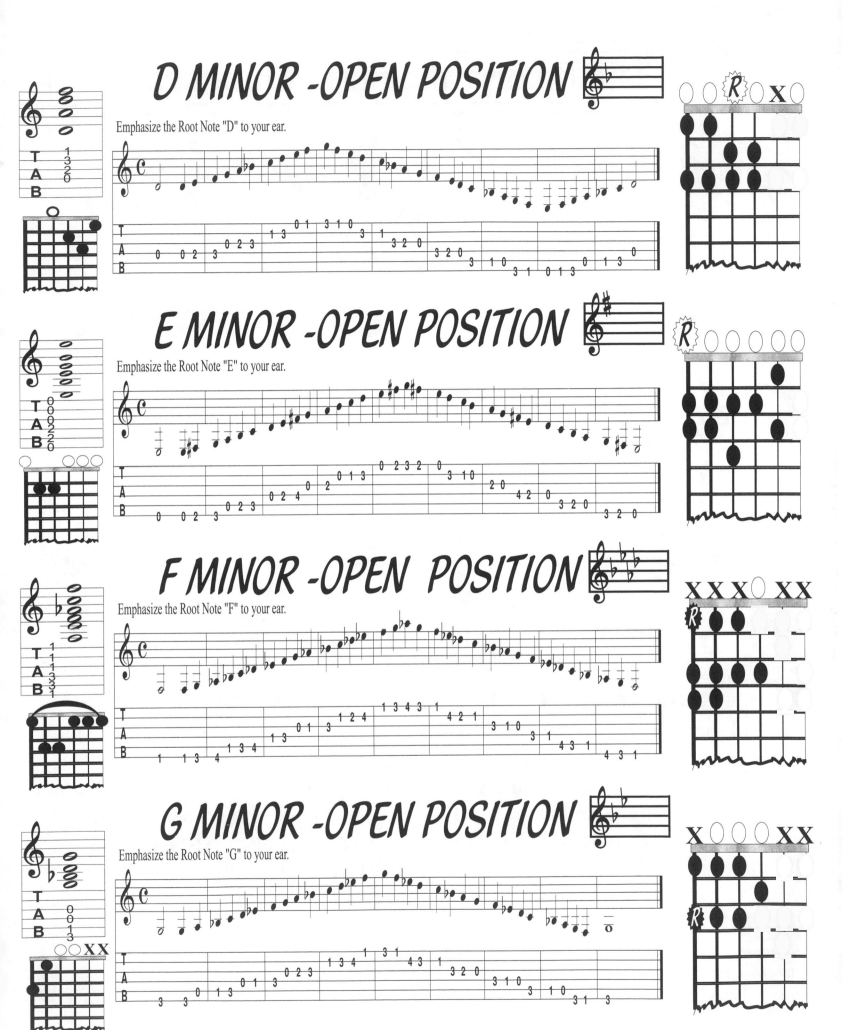

D MINOR -OPEN POSITION

Emphasize the Root Note "D" to your ear.

E MINOR -OPEN POSITION

Emphasize the Root Note "E" to your ear.

F MINOR -OPEN POSITION

Emphasize the Root Note "F" to your ear.

G MINOR -OPEN POSITION

Emphasize the Root Note "G" to your ear.

Major ☯ minor

Bright
Happy
Strong
Consonant
Powerful
Triumphant
Melodic

MELODIES solos solos MELODIES

Dark
Sad
Mysterious
Mornful
Ancient
Ethnic
Melodic

The pure

minor scale (a.k.a. the *natural* or *aeolian* minor) is the second most useful and valuable scale for a musician to know after the Major scale. A 'hands on' interactive approach to the 6 preceding pages *(pp 94-99)* will yield an education in the sound or meaning of what we'll call **THE** minor scale. The formula, sound and feel of the minor scale should be clear at this point. Reinforce your overall concept by reviewing pages **32-34** and **45-51** Finally, give a listen to some classic tunes based on a minor scale before continuing with the rest of the theory concerning the minor scale.

ROCK	JAZZ	BLUES
Stairway to Heaven	*My Funny Valentine*	*Help Me*
All Along the Watchtower	*Puttin on the Ritz*	*I'll Play the Blues 4 U*
Black Magic Woman	*Song for my Father*	*The Thrill is Gone*
I Shot the Sheriff	*Softly, as in a Morning Sunrise*	
Secret Agent Man	*Europa*	
House of the Rising Sun		

All scales in music derive their particular sounds from the distances separating their notes. This is called a *scale formula.* The **CHROMATIC SCALE** (see page 32), for example, has a distance of a half step between each one of its notes.

A *A#/Bb* B C *C#/Db* D *D#/Eb* E F *F#/Gb* G *G#/Ab* A

$\frac{1}{2}$ $\frac{1}{2}$ $\frac{1}{2}$ $\frac{1}{2}$ $\frac{1}{2}$ $\frac{1}{2}$ $\frac{1}{2}$ $\frac{1}{2}$ $\frac{1}{2}$ $\frac{1}{2}$ $\frac{1}{2}$ $\frac{1}{2}$

G A B C D E F G A B C

The formula for the **CHROMATIC SCALE** is expressed as:
"half, half, half, half, half, half, half, half, half, half, half, half "

The formula for a **MINOR SCALE** is expressed as:
"whole, half, whole, whole, half, whole, whole"

Play an A minor scale by:
1.) Sliding up String 5, the "A" string. »»
2.) Playing the white keys on a piano, starting and ending on "A". »»

Half Step.   Half Step.

A B C D E F G A
1 2 3 4 5 6 7 8
Do Re *May* Fa Sol *Lay* *Tay* Do
1 $\frac{1}{2}$ 1 1 $\frac{1}{2}$ 1 1

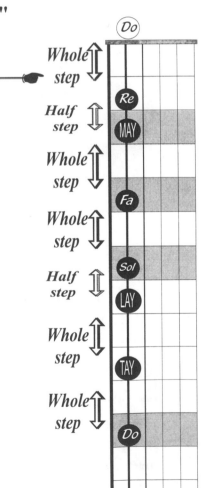

The formula for the minor Scale is expressed as
"whole, half, whole, whole, half, whole, whole".

Any note in the chromatic scale can be the root of its own minor scale. It's possible to build twelve **(and only twelve)** separate and distinct minor scales using the notes of the chromatic scale. Each new and unique minor scale is of course, said to be a *"new key"*. There are twelve separate and distinct minor scales in the language of music.

Every 8 note minor scale contains all seven letters of the musical alphabet with the first *(and last)* note of the scale being the **root note**. In order to play *(and hear)* a minor Scale starting on the **"E"**, note we would first need the letters **"E F G A B C D E"**. According to the Scale formula the interval separating the **2nd & 3rd** notes must be a half step. That being the case, the type of **"F"** note we use must be an **"F#"**, not a plain old **"F"**.

The correct *spelling* of an E minor scale is:

E F# G A B C D E

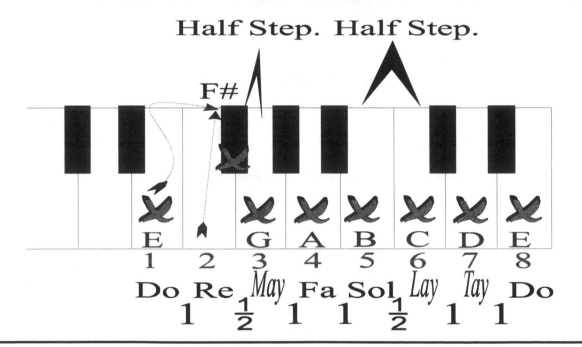

The interval separating notes 5 & 6 (**'B' & 'C'**) is already one of the naturally occurring half steps of the chromatic scale.

There is however, a demand for note 2, **'F'** to be sharped in order to preserve the formula *and sound* of the minor Scale. If you construct a minor Scale with a root note of **"E"**, there is one sharp needed **(F#)** in order to make it come out with the right sound. This is what is meant by the following statement:

"The key of E minor has one sharp"

One octave of ANY MINOR SCALE contains eight notes. Half steps separate the 2ND
and 3RD notes and also the 5TH and 6TH notes.

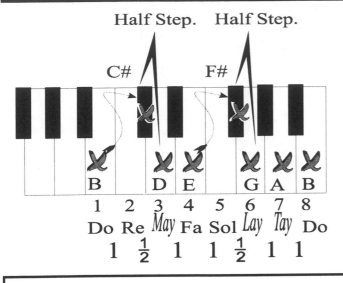

To construct a minor scale with a root
note of **"B"**, we first need to have these notes:

B C D E F G A B.

The *minor scale formula* states that the
interval separating notes **2 & 3**
and also notes **5 & 6** must be a half step.
That being the case, the type of "F" note we
must use is **"F sharp"** and not **"F natural"**.
Accordingly, use **"C Sharp"**,
not **"C natural"**.

The correct *spelling* of a B minor scale is

B C# D E F# G A B

Each new minor scale we construct is the basis of its own system of playing and
composing called a *minor key*.

The two keys we have studied so far *(the keys of "B minor" & "E minor")* are called
sharp keys because they need to use sharped notes to have the correct formula
-and therefore sound- of their own, individual minor scale.

Flat Keys

Some keys need to use flatted notes to have the correct formula and sound of their
own Major scale. They key of **"D minor"** is an example of a *flat key*.

To construct a D minor scale, we must start and end with the note **"D"** and have
every other letter of the musical alphabet represented once:

D E F G A B C D.

The interval separating **E & F** (notes 2&3) is a one of the naturally occurring half
steps of the chromatic scale and therefore the addition of flats or sharps is not needed.

The theory of the minor scale states that the interval separating notes 5 & 6
(**"A"** & **"B"**) must be a half step. The sixth note of the scale, **"B"**, must then be flatted.
(Bb). It's incorrect to call this note **"A#"** because a note named **"A"** is already included
in the spelling.

The correct *spelling* of the D minor scale is:

D E F G A B*b* C D

Minor Scale

Sharp Keys

1	2	3	4	5	6	7	8/1
Do	Re	*May*	Fa	Sol	*Lay*	*Tay*	Do

half step *half step*

A	B	C	D	E	F	G	A	Key of A mi: *No Sharps*

E	F#	G	A	B	C	D	E	Key of E mi: *1 Sharp*

B	C#	D	E	F#	G	A	B	Key of B mi: *2 Sharps*

F#	G#	A	B	C#	D	E	F#	Key of F# mi: *3 Sharps*

C#	D#	E	F#	G#	A	B	C#	Key of C# mi: *4 Sharps*

G#	A	B	C#	D#	E	F#	G#	Key of G# mi: *5 Sharps*

D#	E#	F#	G#	A#	B	C#	D#	Key of D# mi: *6 Sharps*

memorize the notes in every key

write out the notes in every key

play in every key

copy the reference charts & hang them up.

These **'sharp keys'** need to use sharped notes to create the sound of their own minor Scale.

104

Reference Charts

Flat Keys

1	2	3	4	5	6	7	8/1
Do	Re	*May*	Fa	Sol	*Lay*	*Tay*	Do

half step ⌄   *half step* ⌄

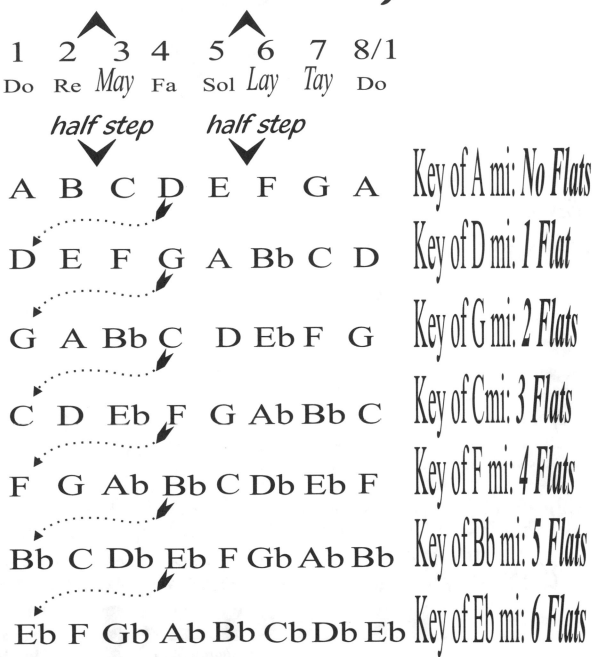

| A | B | C | D | E | F | G | A |

Key of A mi: *No Flats*

| D | E | F | G | A | Bb | C | D |

Key of D mi: *1 Flat*

| G | A | Bb | C | D | Eb | F | G |

Key of G mi: *2 Flats*

| C | D | Eb | F | G | Ab | Bb | C |

Key of C mi: *3 Flats*

| F | G | Ab | Bb | C | Db | Eb | F |

Key of F mi: *4 Flats*

| Bb | C | Db | Eb | F | Gb | Ab | Bb |

Key of Bb mi: *5 Flats*

| Eb | F | Gb | Ab | Bb | Cb | Db | Eb |

Key of Eb mi: *6 Flats*

Play a minor scale in every key.

write in every key

practice in every key

memorize these charts

| G | A | B | C | D | E | F | G | A | B | C |

These **'flat keys'** need to use flatted notes to create the sound of their own minor Scale.

Theory of Relativity

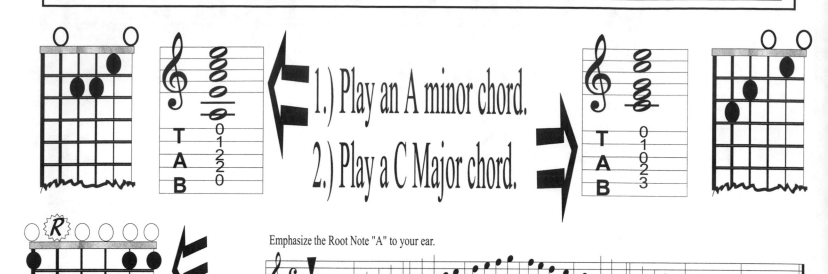

1.) Play an A minor chord.

2.) Play a C Major chord.

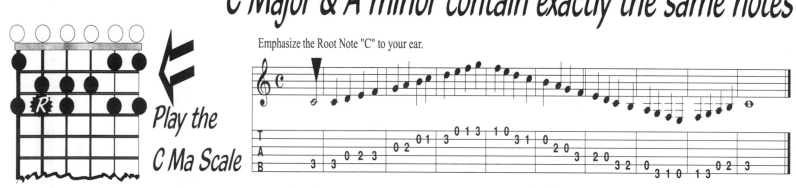

Play the A mi Scale

Emphasize the Root Note "A" to your ear.

C Major & A minor contain exactly the same notes

Play the C Ma Scale

Emphasize the Root Note "C" to your ear.

When a Major scale & a minor scale contain exactly the same notes they are said to be RELATIVES:

A MINOR IS THE RELATIVE MINOR OF C MAJOR

C MAJOR IS THE RELATIVE MAJOR OF A MINOR

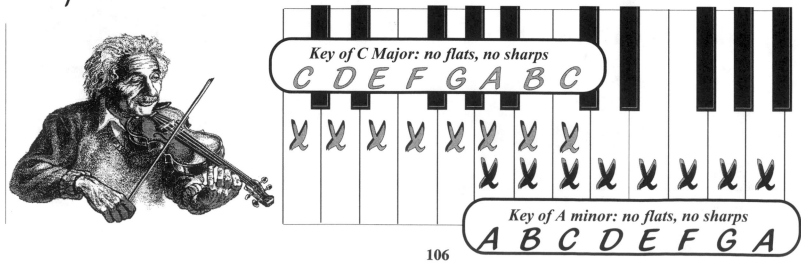

Key of C Major: no flats, no sharps

C D E F G A B C

Key of A minor: no flats, no sharps

A B C D E F G A

Any one of the 12 Major scales in music can be transformed to a minor scale by flatting the **3rd, 6th & 7th** degrees of the scale:

The C Major scale :							
Do	Re	Mi	Fa	Sol	La	Ti	Do
1	**2**	**3**	**4**	**5**	**6**	**7**	**8**
C	**D**	**E**	**F**	**G**	**A**	**B**	**C**

The C minor scale :							
Do	Re	*May*	Fa	Sol	*Lay*	*Tay*	Do
1	**2**	**b3**	**4**	**5**	**b6**	**b7**	**8**
C	**D**	**E**b	**F**	**G**	**A**b	**B**b	**C**

C Major is called the **PARALLEL MAJOR** of *C minor*
C Major is called the **RELATIVE MAJOR** of *A minor*

Any one of the 12 Major scales has a
RELATIVE MINOR .

TWO OCTAVES OF THE C MAJOR SCALE:

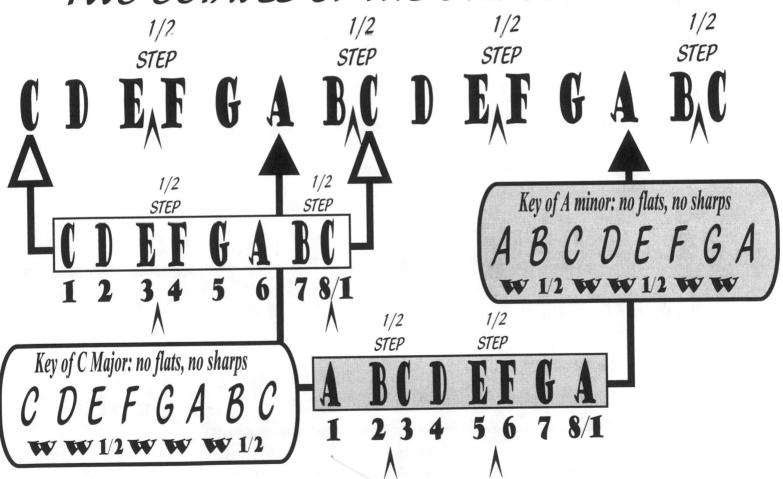

C Major is called the **RELATIVE MAJOR** of *A minor*
A minor is called the **RELATIVE MINOR** of *C Major.*

ANY MAJOR SCALE HAS A RELATE MINOR

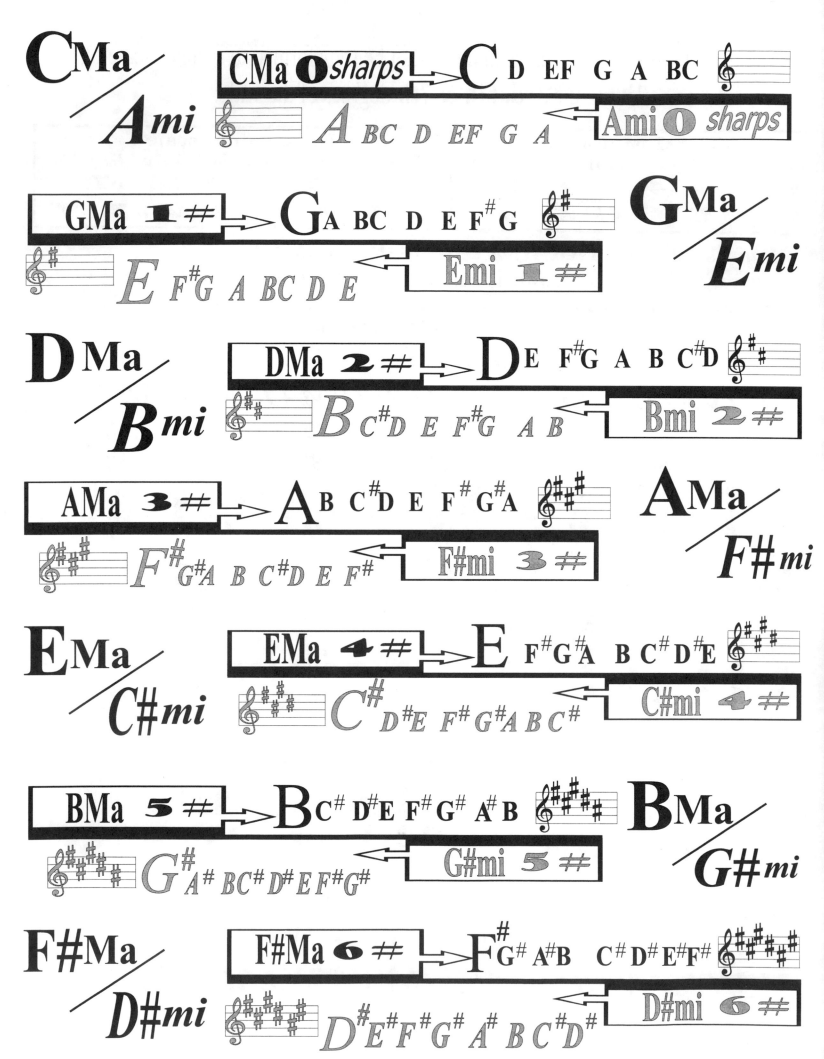

108

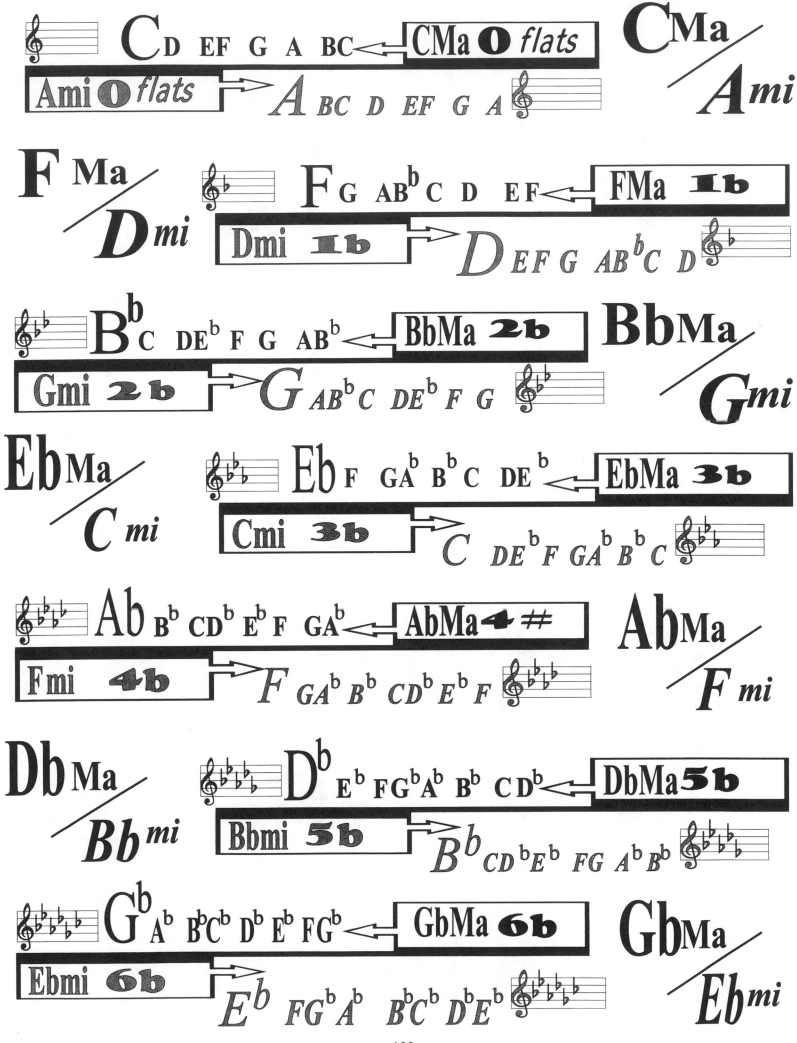

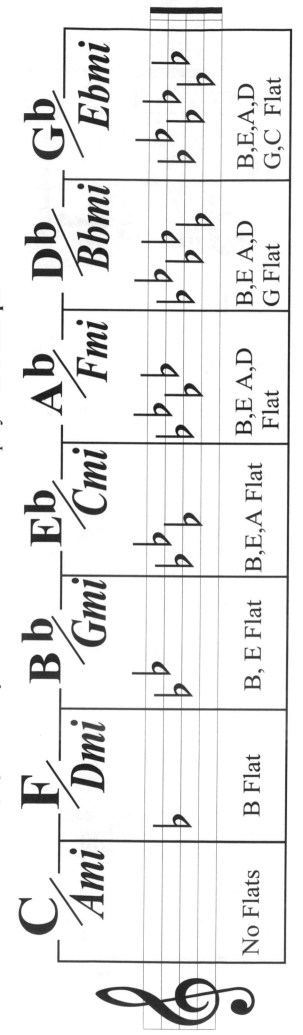

The staffs on this page illustrate the 12 *Key Signatures*. Each one of the 12 keys, or Major scales has a unique *Key Signature*. The *Key Signature* contains the same amount of Flats or Sharps as the corresponding **Major scale.** The *Key Signature* always appears at the beginning of a piece of music to tell you what key the song is written in. Being able to recognize any key signature instantly will tell you the not only the key, but what specific **Major scale** patterns to center your thinking around.

The Key of G (*Relative to and therefore having the same notes as E mi*), has one sharped note: **"F."** The *Key Signature* for the **Key of G** has a sharp symbol placed of the line an **"F"** note might occupy. This means all the music to follow was written in the **Key of G**, the key in which all **"F"** notes are played as **F sharps.**

C/Ami	G/Emi	D/Bmi	A/F#mi	E/C#mi	B/G#mi	F#/D#mi
No Sharps	F Sharp	F, C Sharp	F, C, G Sharp	F, C, G, D Sharp	F, C, G, D, A Sharp	F, C, G, D, A, E Sharp

C/Ami	F/Dmi	Bb/Gmi	Eb/Cmi	Ab/Fmi	Db/Bbmi	Gb/Ebmi
No Flats	B Flat	B, E Flat	B,E,A Flat	B,E A,D Flat	B,E A,D G Flat	B,E,A,D G,C Flat

110

Key of C, Key of Ami
No flats / No sharps

Key of G,
Key of Emi

Key of F,
Key of Dmi   1♭   F

Key of Bb,
Key of Gmi   2♭   B♭

Key of Eb,
Key of C mi   3♭   E♭

Key of Ab,
Key of F mi   4♭   A♭

Key of Db,
Key of Bb mi   5♭   D♭

Key of Gb,
Key of Eb mi   6♭   C♭

C

G 1♯

Key of D,
Key of Bmi   **D** 2♯

Key of A,
Key of F♯ mi   **A** 3♯

Key of E,
Key of C♯ mi   **E** 4♯

Key of B,
Key of G♯ mi   **B** 5♯

Key of F♯,
Key of D♯ mi   **F♯** 6♯

Ami
Emi
Dmi
Bmi
Gmi
F♯mi
Cmi
C♯mi
Fmi
G♯mi
Bbmi
D♯mi
Ebmi

Five Positions of the A minor chord

The **A minor Chord Super Pattern** and the five basic chord shapes of an **A minor** chord are illustrated below. Memorize the 5 shapes of a minor chord and how to play them in each one of the 12 keys. Associating each one of these chord shapes with a scale pattern is an excellent way to make scale playing easy.
GUITAR CHORD GURU -*The Chord Book*, from Creative Concepts is an excellent chord study.

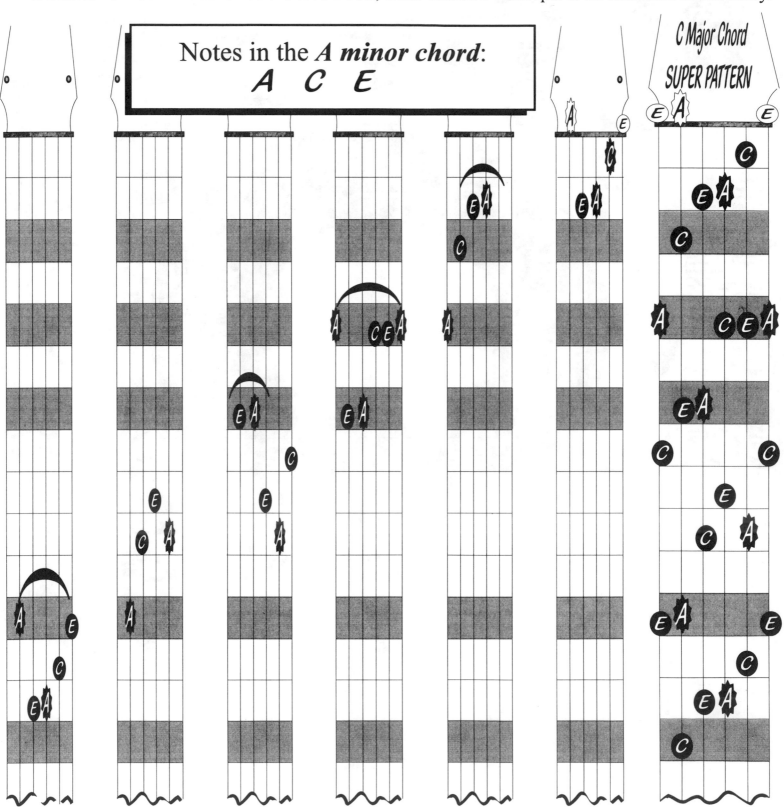

Notes in the *A minor chord*:
A C E

C Major Chord
SUPER PATTERN

Five Positions of the A Minor Scale.

The **A minor Scale Super Pattern** yields five successive connected scale shapes on the guitar. Learn the 5 minor scale patterns and how to play them in each one of the 12 keys. I suggest mentally linking each scale pattern with one of the 5 basic chord shapes.

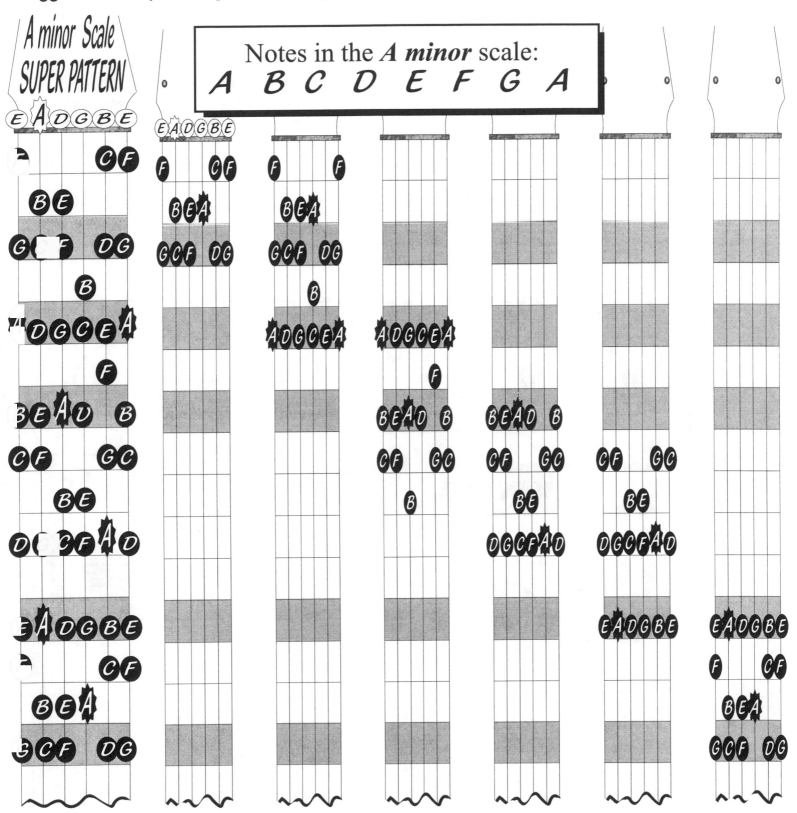

Notes in the *A minor* scale:
A B C D E F G A

The Linking System: Minor Scales

Learning to play an A minor scale in five logical interconnected positions involves thinking in terms of 5 minor chord voicings in the open position:

Ami   Gmi   Emi   Dmi   Cmi

    Each one of the 5 chords in this system is thought of as movable chord. By moving these chords up the neck, its possible to play each one of the 5 minor chords with a root note of **"A"**. For example, when every note in a basic **E minor** chord is raised in pitch by five frets the resulting chord is **A minor,** which has a shape and appearance just like the plain old **E minor** chord we started out with except for the fact that's its now on the fifth fret. Organizing the guitar in terms of 5 open string chords (C, A, G, E, D) in this manner is called the **CAGED SYSTEM.**

    If its possible to play 5 different versions of an **A minor chord,** then its also possible to play 5 different versions of an **A minor scale.** I've found that associating each one of the 5 **"Ami"** chords with its own individual fingering for an **A minor scale** is a powerful learning tool.

I call this **THE LINKING SYSTEM.**

A Minor -open position

Ami type — Associate this scale, in this position with an A minor type of chord. In this case, the chord type we link the scale to is actually one of the 5 basic open position chords.

LINK WITH → A minor -Open Position

A minor - second position

Gmi type

Associate the A minor scale, in position II with an **G minor type of chord**: when a basic open string G minor is moved up the neck *(higher in pitch)* 2 frets the result is an A minor chord, position II.

Gmi

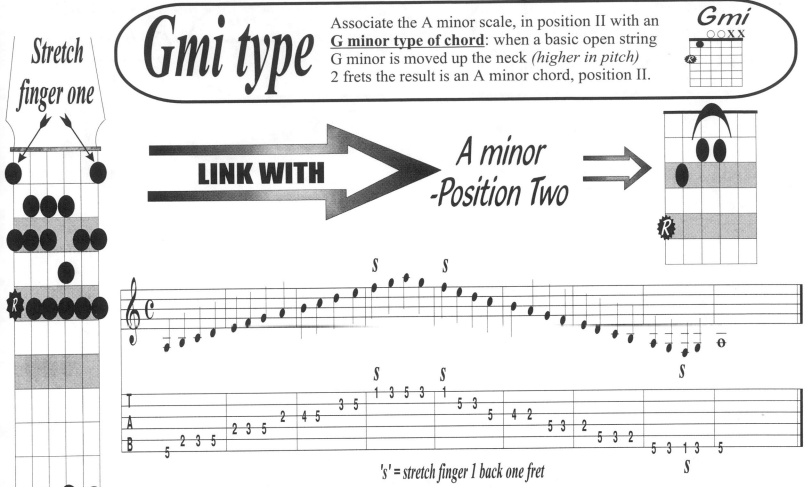

Stretch finger one

LINK WITH ➡ **A minor -Position Two** ➡

's' = stretch finger 1 back one fret

Optional A minor scale -Positions II & III

LINK WITH ➡ **A minor -Second Position**

The sliding version of an A minor scale pictured at left is a favorite among guitarists in need of an A minor scale in position two.

Although this position shifting idea is smooth and comfortable, I strongly urge you to master the stretching approach to scale playing as your first line of thinking.

position II

position III

position II

115

A minor -fifth position

Emi type Associate the A minor scale, in position V with a E **minor type of chord**: when a basic open string E minor chord is moved up the neck *(higher in pitch)* 5 frets the result is a A minor, position V.

E mi

A minor -Fifth Position

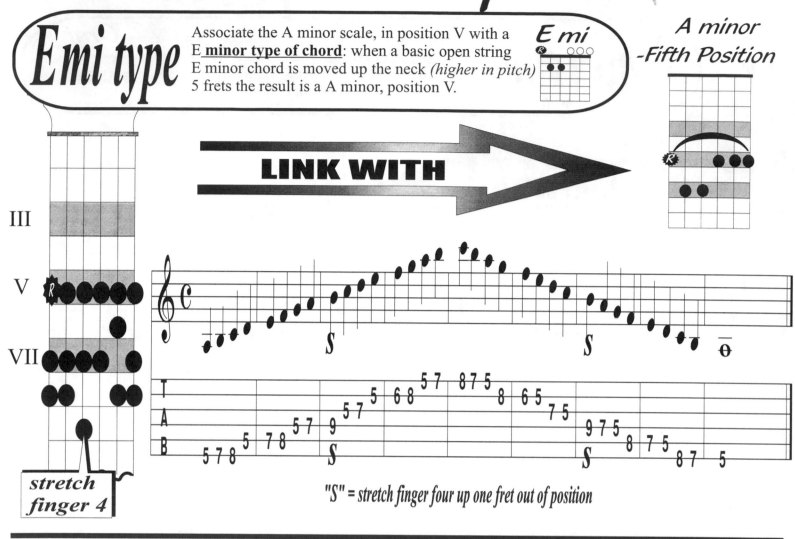

LINK WITH

III

V

VII

stretch finger 4

"S" = stretch finger four up one fret out of position

Optional A minor scale -Positions IV & V

A minor -Fifth Position

LINK WITH

The "CAGED" system contains several areas of variability. There is no right or wrong implied here -just two useful ways.
Again, I recommend you use the 'stretching' version as your first line of thought. Of course master the 'sliding' version illustrated at left.

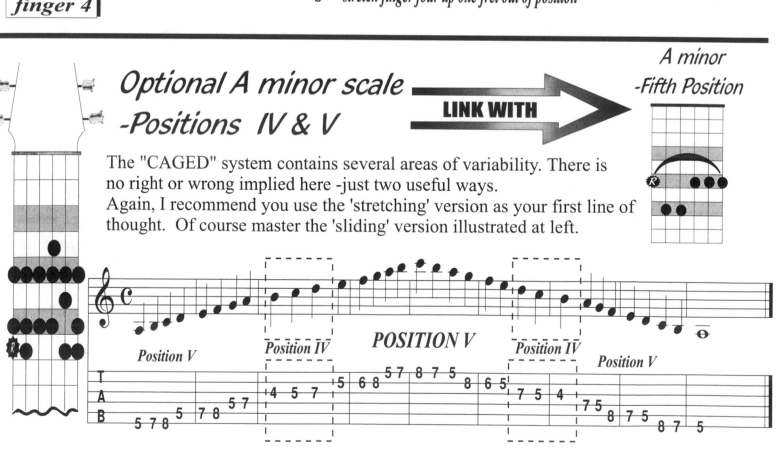

Position V   Position IV   *POSITION V*   Position IV   Position V

A minor -seventh position

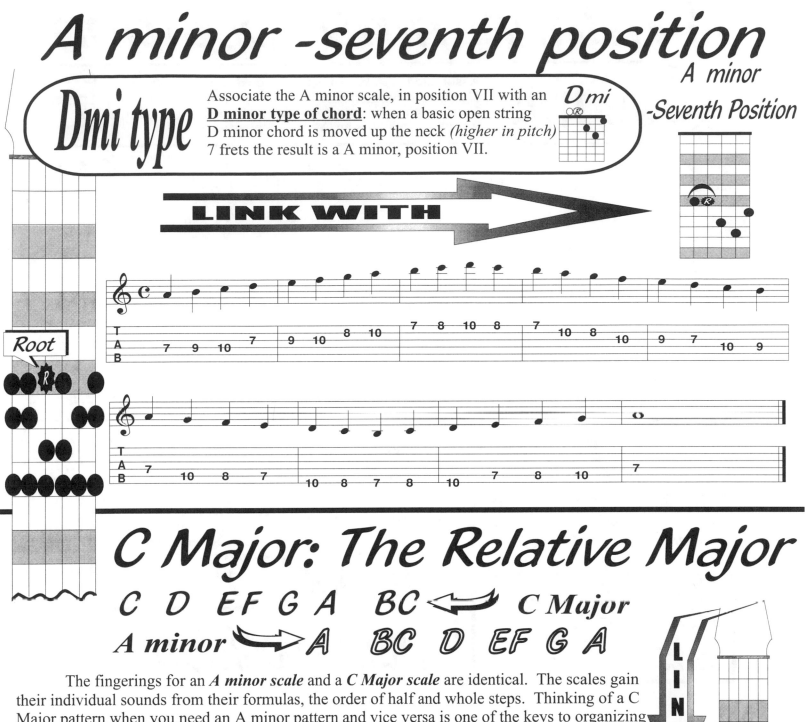

Dmi type

Associate the A minor scale, in position VII with an **D minor type of chord**: when a basic open string D minor chord is moved up the neck *(higher in pitch)* 7 frets the result is a A minor, position VII.

Dmi

A minor -Seventh Position

LINK WITH

Root

C Major: The Relative Major

C D EF G A BC ⟵ C Major

A minor ⟶ A BC D EF G A

LINK

C Major -Eighth Position

The fingerings for an *A minor scale* and a *C Major scale* are identical. The scales gain their individual sounds from their formulas, the order of half and whole steps. Thinking of a C Major pattern when you need an A minor pattern and vice versa is one of the keys to organizing your thoughts concerning scale playing.

It's absolutely essential for a guitarist to have memorized all 12 keys and their relative minors (see pp. 106-111). It makes finding scales and therefore playing in key much easier.

Take the sixth

The sixth note of a C Major scale is *"A"*. For all Major scales, the relative minor begins on the sixth note *(La)* of the scale. Try saying the solfege syllables *(Do, Re, Mi, Fa, Sol, La, Ti, Do)* when blowing through your Major scales. Many of my students have found this makes learning the minor scales much easier because it give them the ability to compare these "new" scales to the finely tuned Major scales they have worked so hard to commit to memory. By learning how to play *C Major (Do)* you automically learn to play *A minor (La)*. Knowing any Major scale *(Do)* means you also know its relative minor *(La)*.

Learn the Key of A minor as its own entity, according to the **CAGED** system as I've described beginning on page 112. As you continue to master the sound and feel of the 5 separate A minor scales make the mental connection to the C Major scale in the same position. Every *Major scale* you learn is also a *minor scale,* every *minor scale* you learn is also a *Major scale*. Looking at scales in this manner is an excellent way to learn not only the guitar, but music in general.

A minor -ninth position

Cmi type

Associate the A minor scale, in position IX with an **C minor type of chord**: when a basic open string C minor chord is moved up the neck *(higher in pitch)* 9 frets the result is an A minor, position IX.

Cmi

III
V
VII
XII

"s" = stretch finger one back - one fret out of position to fret VIII

LINK WITH → A minor Position 9

POSITION NINE

Fret	*VIII*	IX	X	XI	XII
Finger	*1*	1	2	3	4

VIII IX X XI XII
1 2 3 4

STRETCH FINGER 1 BACK TO FRET EIGHT

A minor -multi position

Remember:
To play a scale pattern which covers **5 frets** with **4 fingers** you must;
A.) Stretch
B.) Shift

LINK WITH →

Starting Note: Fret XII, FINGER 3

III
V
VII
XII

Position X   Position IX   Position X

Position IX   Position X

118

A minor -twelfth position

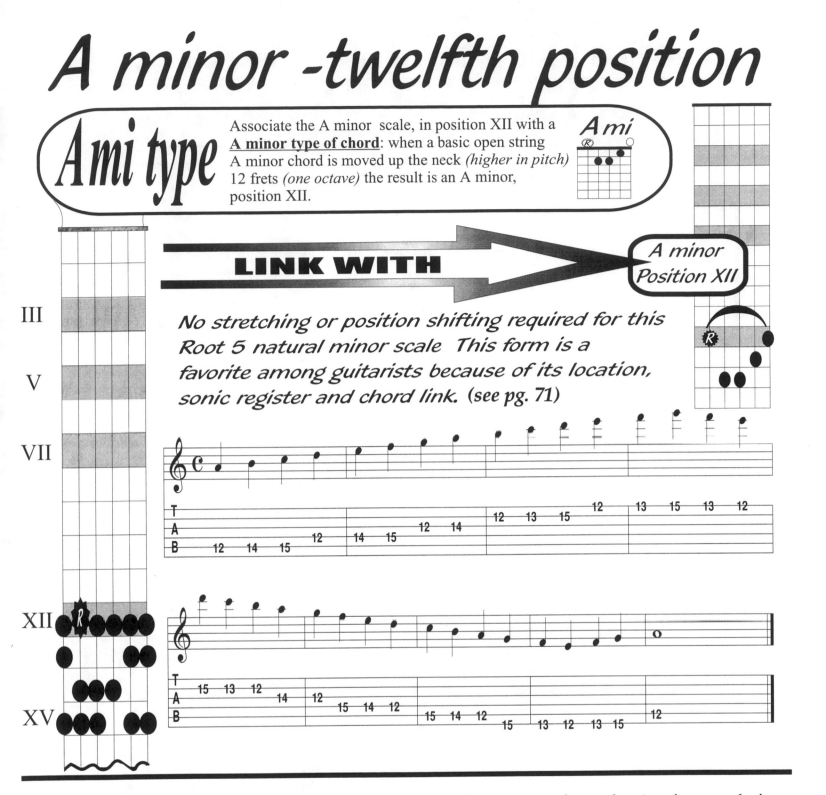

Ami type

Associate the A minor scale, in position XII with a **A minor type of chord**: when a basic open string A minor chord is moved up the neck *(higher in pitch)* 12 frets *(one octave)* the result is an A minor, position XII.

A mi

LINK WITH

A minor Position XII

No stretching or position shifting required for this Root 5 natural minor scale This form is a favorite among guitarists because of its location, sonic register and chord link. (see pg. 71)

III

V

VII

XII

XV

The A minor scale in position XII is exactly the same scale as the A minor scale in the open position *(see pp. 97 & pp. 98)* except one octave higher. Of course, any open strings are changed to twelfth fret notes. The scale fingerings have completely covered the neck in the key of A minor and begin to repeat themselves in the same order.

I've suggested mentally associating each new scale shape with a chord form. I call this **THE LINKING SYSTEM** and it makes finding and remembering various chords and scales much easier.

Good soloists understand the hand in hand relationship between chords and scales. Make sure you can play five positions of a *Major, minor* and *dominant* chord for every key. For a study of this check out **The Chord Book** also from Creative Concepts Publishing.

The 5 basic shapes of an A minor chord.

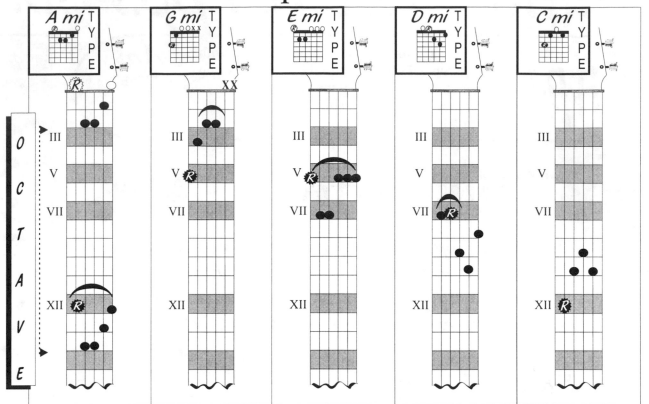

The 5 basic shapes of an A minor scale.

's' -means stretch finger one or four out of position.

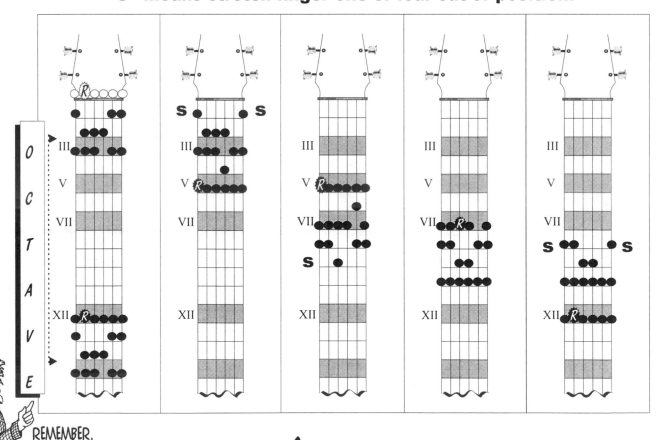

REMEMBER,
   C MAJOR & A MINOR ARE RELATIVES
THEY CONTAIN THE EXACT SAME NOTES AND
SHARE A KEY SIGNATURE

C D EF G A BC → *C Major*

A minor → *A BC D EF G A*

MINOR KEYS

A mi Type

As you learn the 5 basic shapes of every minor Chord * associate a minor scale pattern with each chord shape. The root note of the chord will also be the root note of the scale in your new system of thinking. Every serious guitar student must master this concept.

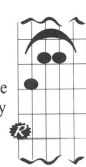

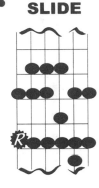

No need to stretch or slide, always **LINK** an *Ami type* of chord to this minor scale fingering. Think of this scale fingering as your *Ami type* of minor scale.

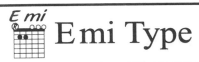

G mi Type

Every scale shape is not as clear and logical as the *A mi type.* If the *G mi type* of scale is to be played strictly in position, you must temporarily stretch the first finger back one fret out of position.

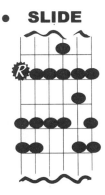

E mi Type

The *E mi type* of minor scale is critical because its linked to **the** Root 6 form of a minor chord. Master the fourth finger stretch but also be able to use the sliding, multi position version.

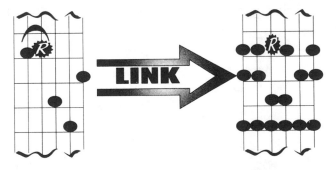

D mi Type

The *D mi type* of minor scale is clearly in position. Because this pattern also doubles as the most used form of a Major scale think of the Relative Major when practicing this and all minor scales.

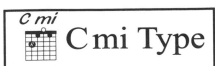

No need to stretch or slide, always **LINK** a *D mi type* of chord to this minor scale fingering. Think of this scale fingering as your *D mi type* of minor scale.

C mi Type

The *C mi type* of chord is linked to two minor scales: First, the version in which finger one stretches on strings 6, 5 & 1. The next shows the method for position switching.

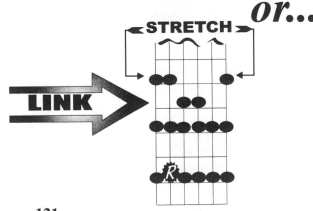

Voicings based upon
"GUITAR CHORD GURU -The Chord Book"

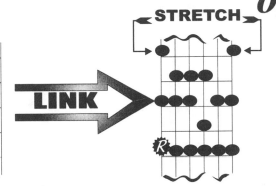

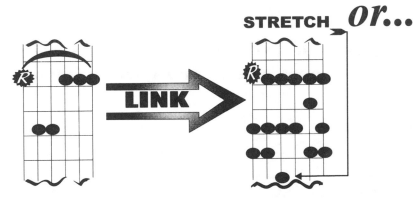

The 5 basic shapes of a C minor chord.

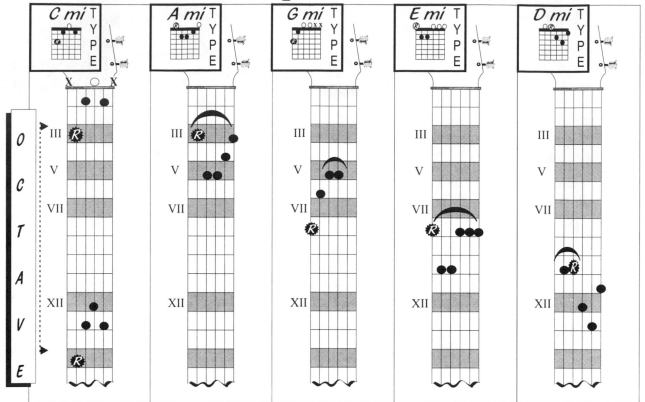

The 5 basic shapes of a C minor scale.

's' -means stretch finger one or four out of position.

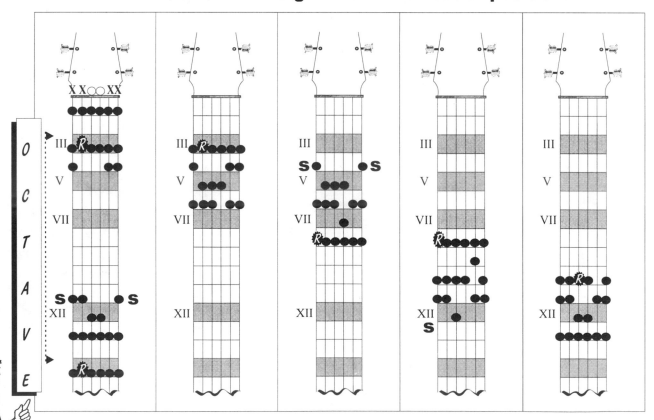

REMEMBER,
   C MINOR & E♭ MAJOR ARE RELATIVES:
THEY CONTAIN THE EXACT SAME NOTES AND
SHARE A KEY SIGNATURE

E♭F GA♭ B♭ C DE♭ ⟵ Eb Major

C minor ⟶ C DE♭F GA♭B♭C

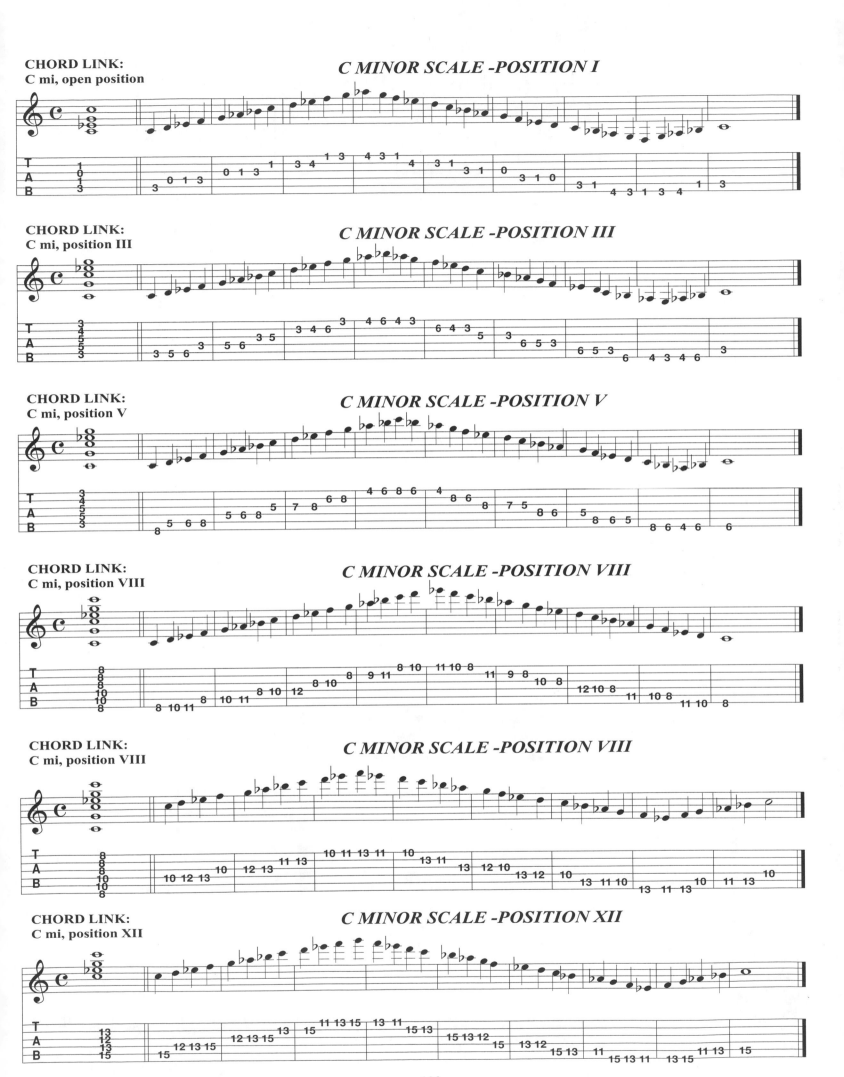

123

The 5 basic shapes of an E minor chord.

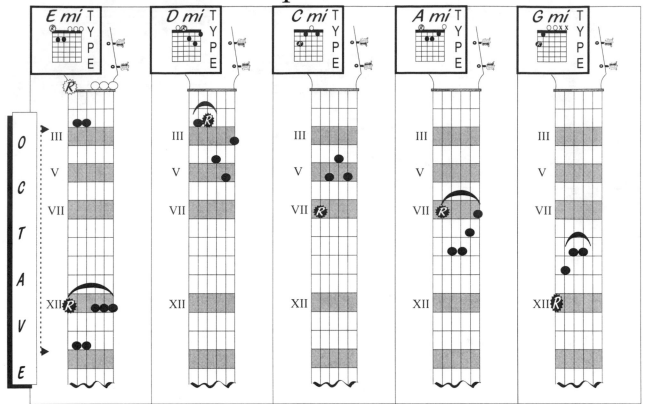

The 5 basic shapes of an E minor scale.

's' -means stretch finger one or four out of position.

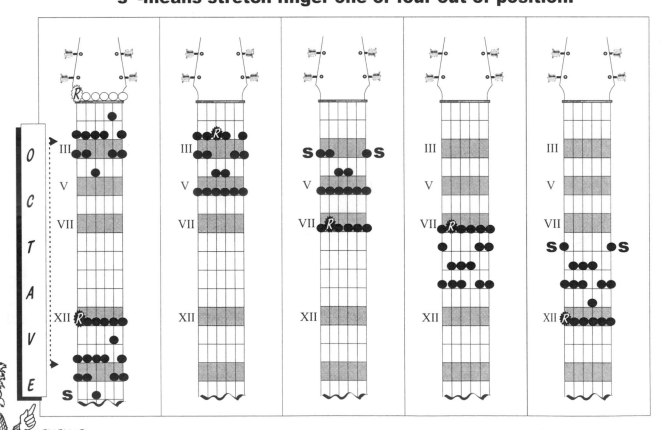

REMEMBER,
E MINOR & G MAJOR ARE RELATIVES
THEY CONTAIN THE EXACT SAME NOTES AND
SHARE A KEY SIGNATURE

E F# G A B C D E ⟵ E minor

G Major ⟶ G A B C D E F G

E MINOR SCALE -OPEN POSITION

E MINOR SCALE -POSITION II

E MINOR SCALE -POSITION IV

E MINOR SCALE -POSITION VII

E MINOR SCALE -POSITION VIII

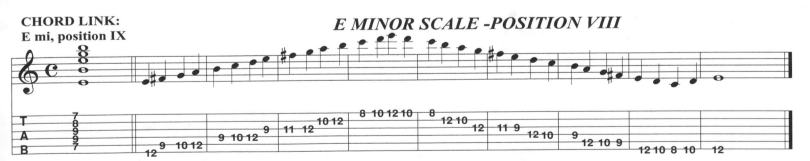

E MINOR SCALE -OPEN POSITION

The 5 basic shapes of a G minor chord.

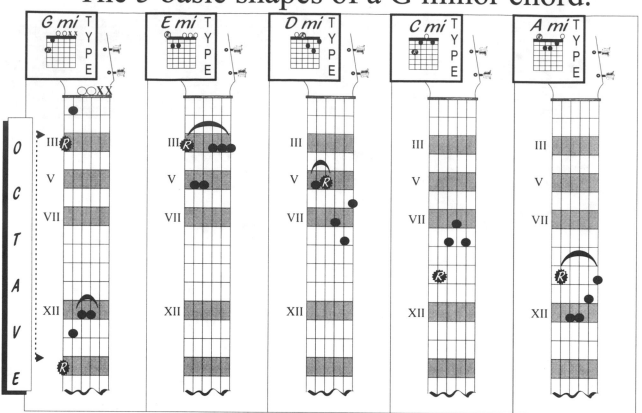

The 5 basic shapes of a G minor scale.

's' -means stretch finger one or four out of position.

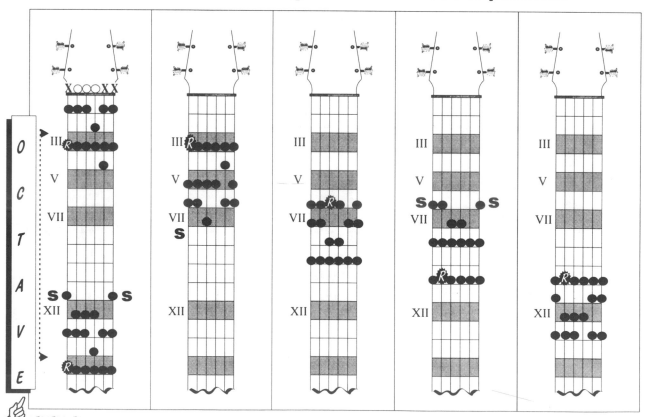

REMEMBER,

B♭ MAJOR & G MINOR ARE RELATIVES
THEY CONTAIN THE EXACT SAME NOTES AND
SHARE A KEY SIGNATURE

B♭ C D E♭ F G A B♭ ⟵ B♭ Major

G minor ⟹ G A B♭ C D E♭ F G

CHORD LINK:
G mi, open position

G MINOR SCALE -OPEN POSITION

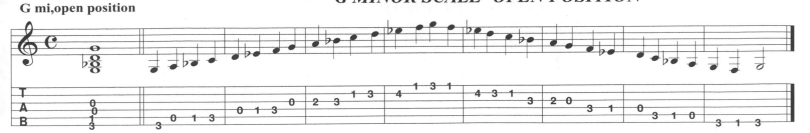

CHORD LINK:
G mi, position III

G MINOR SCALE -POSITION III

CHORD LINK:
G mi, position V

G MINOR SCALE -POSITION VI

CHORD LINK:
G mi, position VII

G MINOR SCALE -POSITION VII

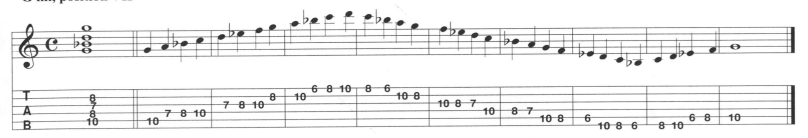

CHORD LINK:
G mi, position X

G MINOR SCALE -POSITION X

CHORD LINK:
G mi, position XII

G MINOR SCALE -POSITION XII

The 5 basic shapes of a D minor chord.

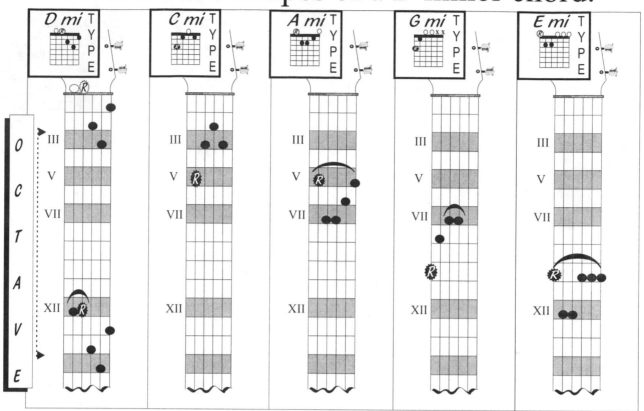

The 5 basic shapes of a D minor scale.

's' -means stretch finger one or four out of position.

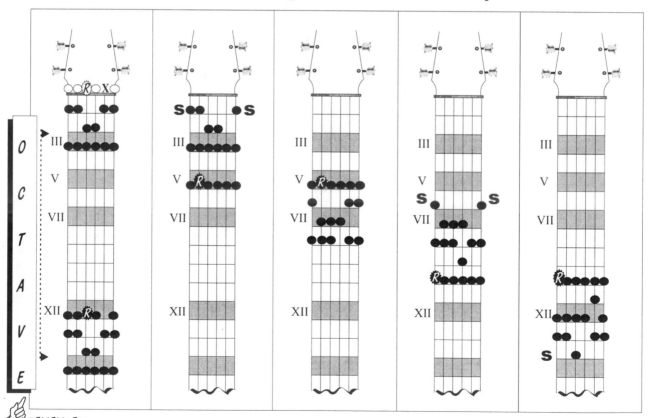

REMEMBER,

F MAJOR & D MINOR ARE RELATIVES
THEY CONTAIN THE EXACT SAME NOTES AND
SHARE A KEY SIGNATURE

F G A B♭ C D E F ⟵ *F Major*

D minor ⟶ D E F G A B♭ C D

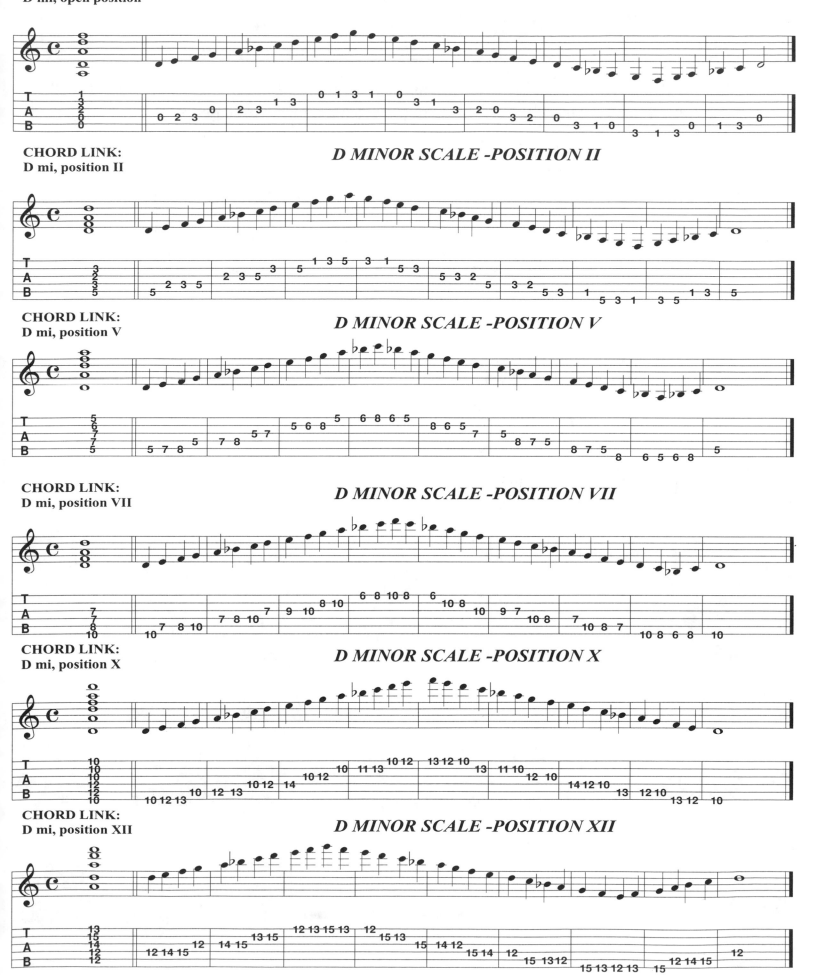

129

Five Position Thinking: Minor Pentatonics

The minor pentatonic scale is the bread and butter of Rock, blues, pop, soul and funk lead guitar playing. Discussions of the minor pentatonic scale appear on pages 52, 56, 68, and 70 of this book. Learn every scale in 5 successive interconnected shapes.

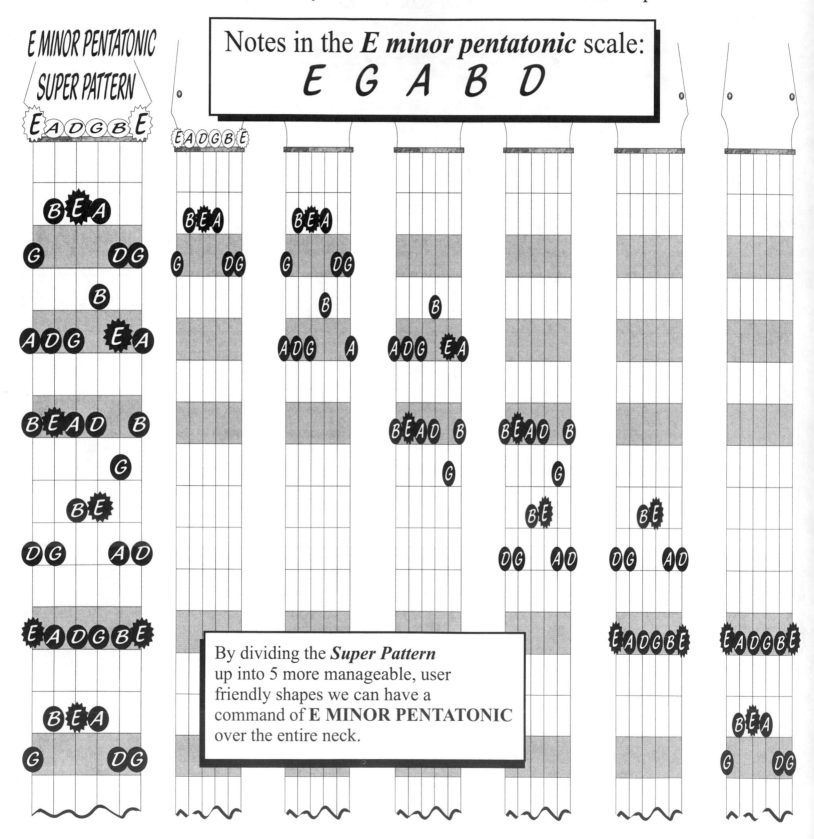

E MINOR PENTATONIC SUPER PATTERN

Notes in the *E minor pentatonic* scale:
E G A B D

By dividing the *Super Pattern* up into 5 more manageable, user friendly shapes we can have a command of **E MINOR PENTATONIC** over the entire neck.

Five Position Thinking: Dominant Chords

Below is a diagram of the **E Dominant 7 Chord Super Pattern** and the five basic shapes of an E7 Chord. Make the mental association between an *E7 chord* and a *E minor pentatonic* scale in each position as illustrated below.

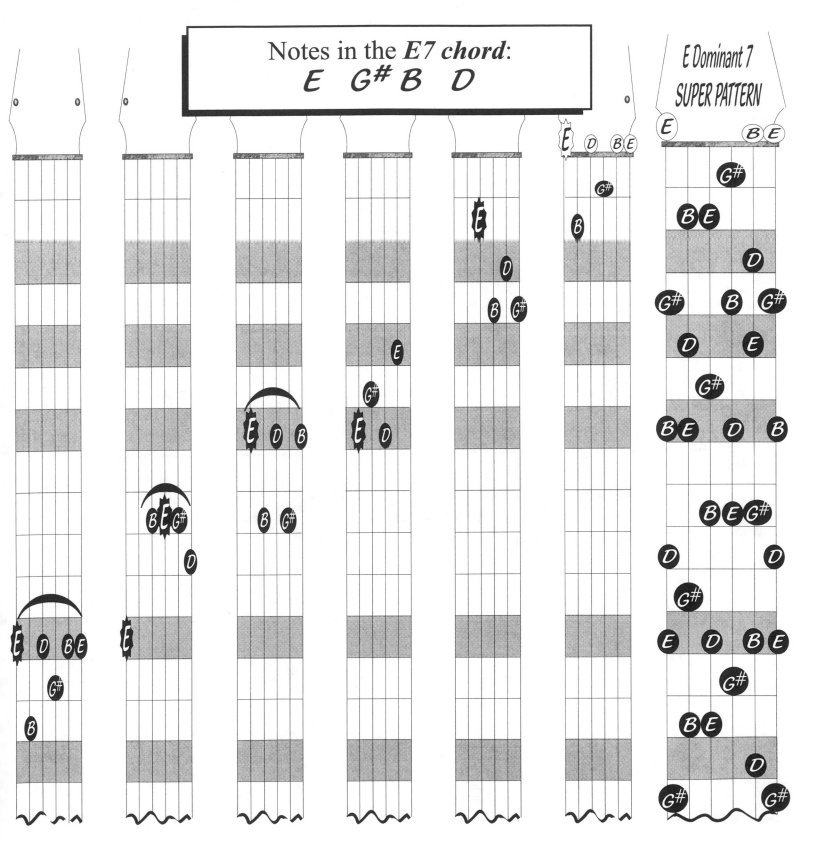

Notes in the *E7 chord*:
E G# B D

E Dominant 7 SUPER PATTERN

The Linking System: Minor Pentatonics.

To learn how to think of and play the 5 MINOR PENTATONIC scales shapes
start with 5 dominant chords in the open position:

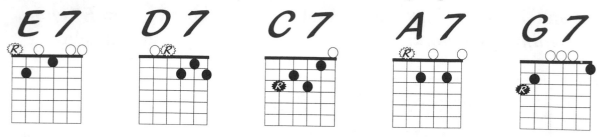

Apply 5 open string chords (*E7, D7, C7, A7, G7*) to the
CAGED SYSTEM. Think of the resulting chords as the
CHORD LINKS as I have illustrated below Associating each
scale form you learn with a corresponding chord
shape makes learning, playing and changing keys much easier.

E MAJOR	1	2	3	4	5	6	7	8/1
	E	F#	G#	A	B	C#	D#	E

E MINOR PENTATONIC	E	G	A	B	D	E
	1	b3	4	5	b7	1

E minor pentatonic -open position

E 7 type

Associate this scale, in this position with **an E7 type of chord**. In this
case, the chord type we link the scale to is in fact one of the 5 basic
open position chords. Of course, an E minor pentatonic scale has many
more applications than just E7. Linking E minor pentatonic to E7 is
only one step in understanding chord/ scale relationships.

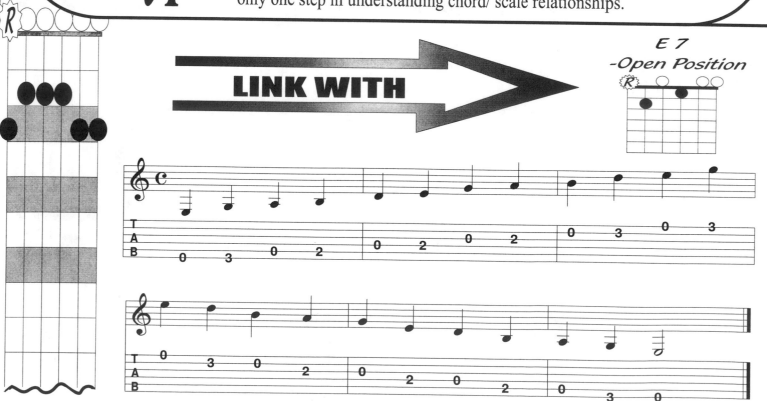

LINK WITH

E 7
-Open Position

E minor pentatonic -second position

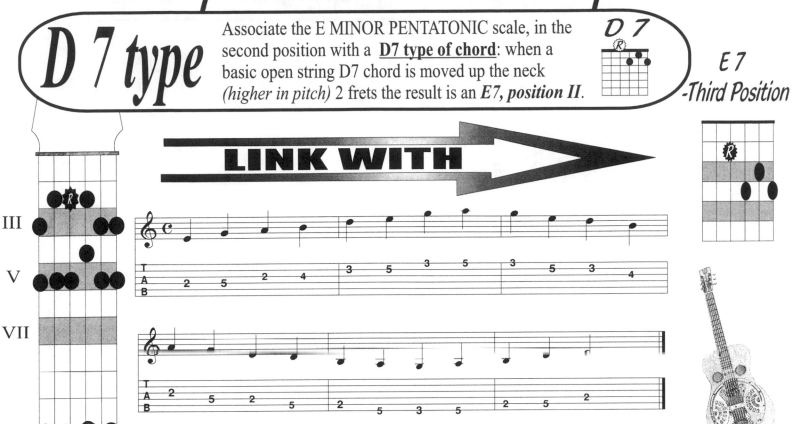

D 7 type

Associate the E MINOR PENTATONIC scale, in the second position with a **D7 type of chord**: when a basic open string D7 chord is moved up the neck *(higher in pitch)* 2 frets the result is an **E7, position II**.

D 7

LINK WITH

E 7 -Third Position

III

V

VII

E minor pentatonic -fifth position

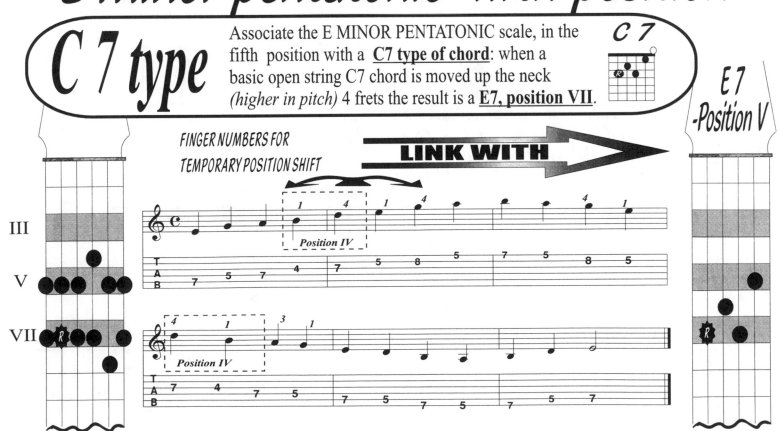

C 7 type

Associate the E MINOR PENTATONIC scale, in the fifth position with a **C7 type of chord**: when a basic open string C7 chord is moved up the neck *(higher in pitch)* 4 frets the result is a **E7, position VII**.

C 7

E 7 -Position V

FINGER NUMBERS FOR TEMPORARY POSITION SHIFT

LINK WITH

Position IV

Position IV

III

V

VII

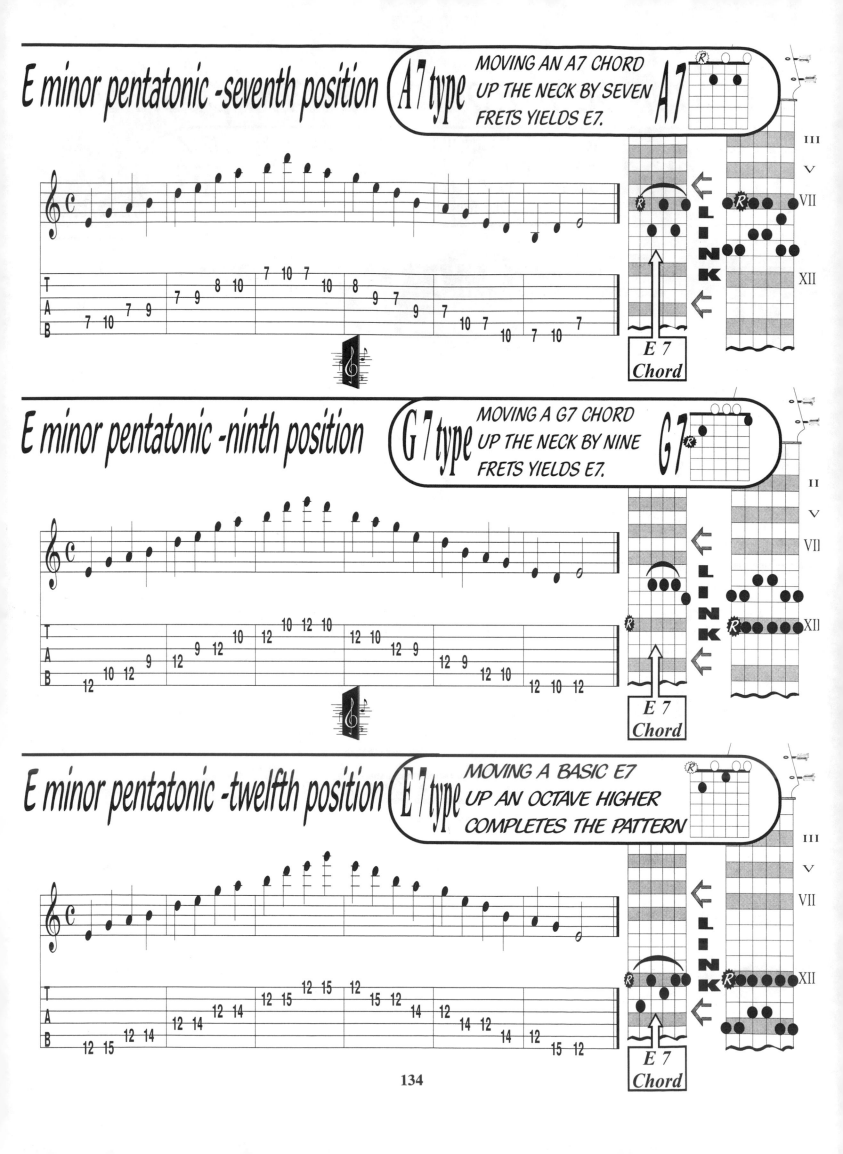

E minor pentatonic -seventh position

A7 type — MOVING AN A7 CHORD UP THE NECK BY SEVEN FRETS YIELDS E7.

E 7 Chord

E minor pentatonic -ninth position

G7 type — MOVING A G7 CHORD UP THE NECK BY NINE FRETS YIELDS E7.

E 7 Chord

E minor pentatonic -twelfth position

E7 type — MOVING A BASIC E7 UP AN OCTAVE HIGHER COMPLETES THE PATTERN

E 7 Chord

Minor Pentatonic Scale Reference Charts

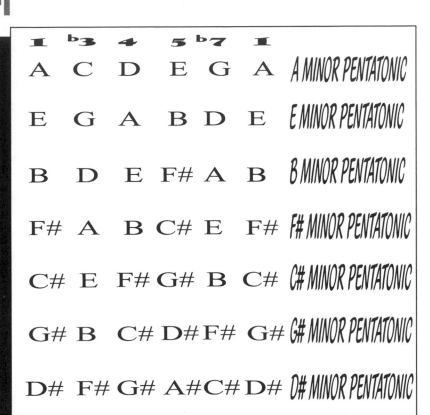

1	b3	4	5	b7	1	
A	C	D	E	G	A	A MINOR PENTATONIC
E	G	A	B	D	E	E MINOR PENTATONIC
B	D	E	F#	A	B	B MINOR PENTATONIC
F#	A	B	C#	E	F#	F# MINOR PENTATONIC
C#	E	F#	G#	B	C#	C# MINOR PENTATONIC
G#	B	C#	D#	F#	G#	G# MINOR PENTATONIC
D#	F#	G#	A#	C#	D#	D# MINOR PENTATONIC

Music theory: The Minor Pentatonic Scale

All discussions of music theory are based on the Major scale which is the foundation and basis of theory. All notes of the major scale are refered to by number. For example, the key of "A":

$$A \quad B \quad C{\#} \quad D \quad E \quad F{\#} \quad G{\#} \quad A$$
$$1 \quad 2 \quad 3 \quad 4 \quad 5 \quad 6 \quad 7 \quad 1$$

The formula for a **MINOR PENTATONIC** scale is:

$$1 \quad {}^{b}3 \quad 4 \quad 5 \quad {}^{b}7$$

The **MINOR PENTATONIC** in the key of "A" is:

$$A \quad (\natural) \quad C \quad D \quad E \quad (\natural) \quad G$$

TWO THINGS:

1.) The note "C#" is the normally occurring third in an **A Major scale.** A flatted third in this case is **"C♮"**-a regular "C" note.

The same thing holds true for the third note of an E Major scale which naturally occurs as a "G#." The flatted third note of a **E Major scale** is therefore **"G♮"** *(G natural).*

2.) Think very hard about how to play every scale in each one of the 12 keys. We haven't diagrammed every scale in every key because the concepts of five movable patterns **(CAGED)** and **THE LINKING SYSTEM** make it possible to play any scale we've studied in five positions for each of the 12 keys. Seeing the illustrations in just a few keys is enough for you to learn how to do this.

	1	b3	4	5	b7	1
A MINOR PENTATONIC	A	C	D	E	G	A
D MINOR PENTATONIC	D	F	G	A	C	D
G MINOR PENTATONIC	G	Bb	C	D	F	G
C MINOR PENTATONIC	C	Eb	F	G	Bb	C
F MINOR PENTATONIC	F	Ab	Bb	C	Eb	F
Bb MINOR PENTATONIC	Bb	Db	Eb	F	Ab	Bb
Eb MINOR PENTATONIC	Eb	Gb	Ab	Bb	Db	Eb

The 5 basic shapes of a G 7 chord.

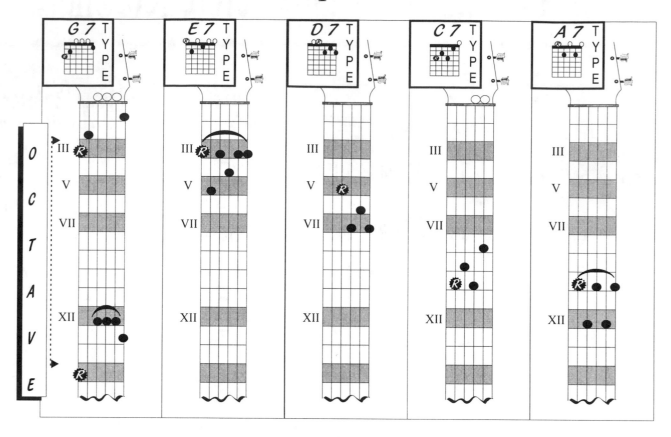

The 5 basic shapes of a G Minor Pentatonic scale.

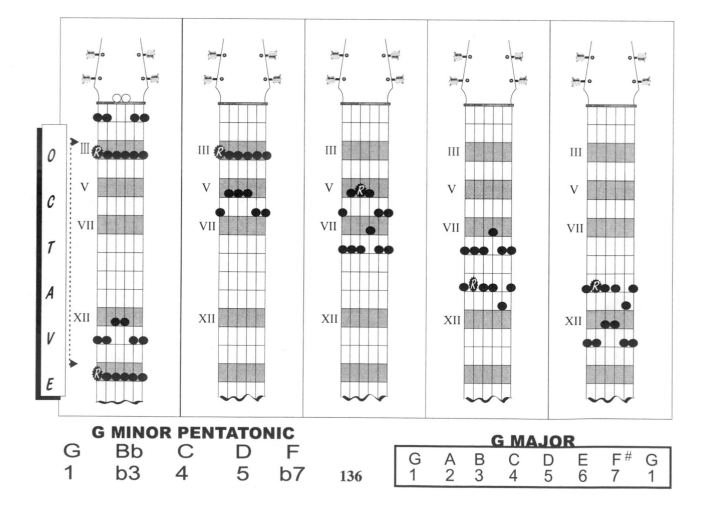

G MINOR PENTATONIC

G	Bb	C	D	F
1	b3	4	5	b7

136

G MAJOR

G	A	B	C	D	E	F#	G
1	2	3	4	5	6	7	1

G MINOR PENTATONIC SCALE -OPEN POSITION

G MINOR PENTATONIC SCALE -POSITION III

G MINOR PENTATONIC SCALE -POSITION V

G MINOR PENTATONIC SCALE -POSITION VIII

Finger numbers

G MINOR PENTATONIC SCALE -POSITION X

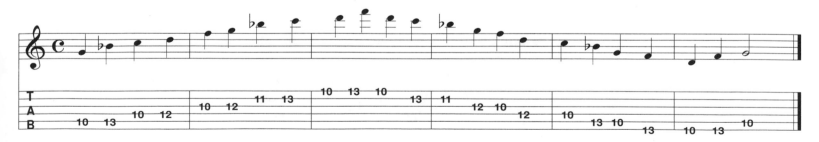

G MINOR PENTATONIC SCALE -POSITION XII

The 5 basic shapes of an A 7 chord.

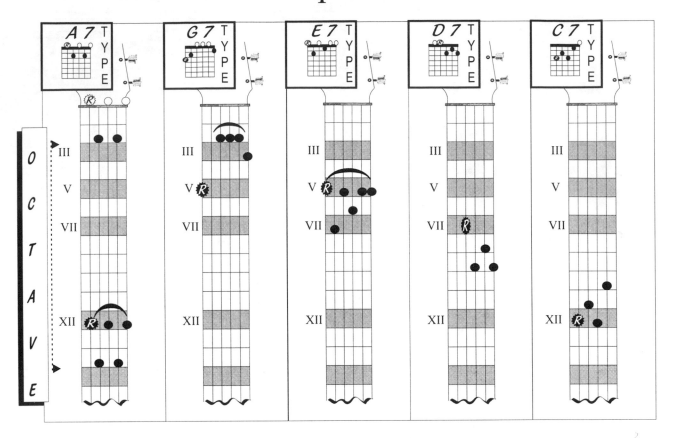

The 5 basic shapes of an A Minor Pentatonic scale.

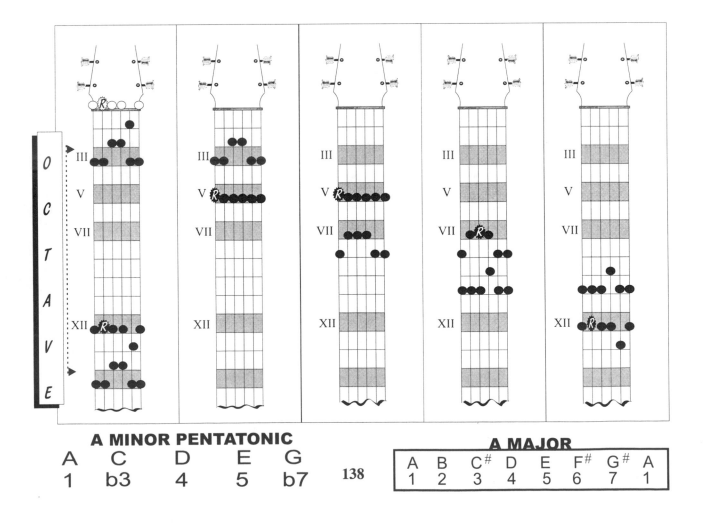

A MINOR PENTATONIC				
A	C	D	E	G
1	b3	4	5	b7

138

A MAJOR							
A	B	C#	D	E	F#	G#	A
1	2	3	4	5	6	7	1

A MINOR PENTATONIC SCALE -OPEN POSITION

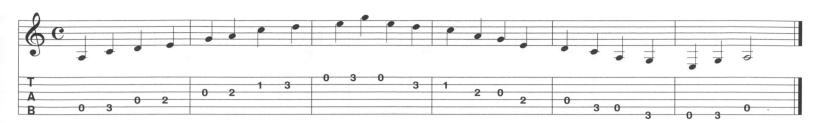

A MINOR PENTATONIC SCALE -POSITION II

A MINOR PENTATONIC SCALE -POSITION V

A MINOR PENTATONIC SCALE -POSITION VII

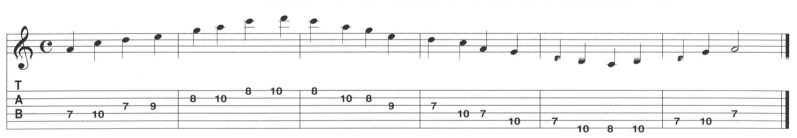

A MINOR PENTATONIC SCALE -POSITION X

A MINOR PENTATONIC SCALE -POSITION XII

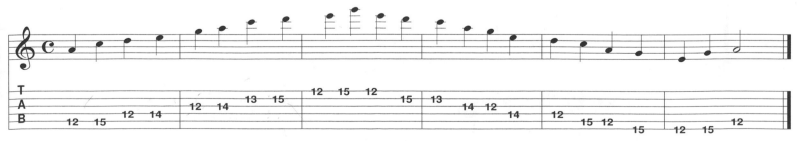

The 5 basic shapes of a C7 chord.

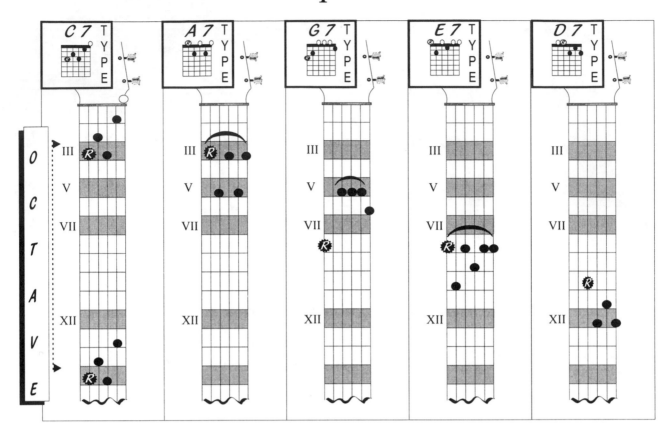

The 5 basic shapes of a C Minor Pentatonic scale.

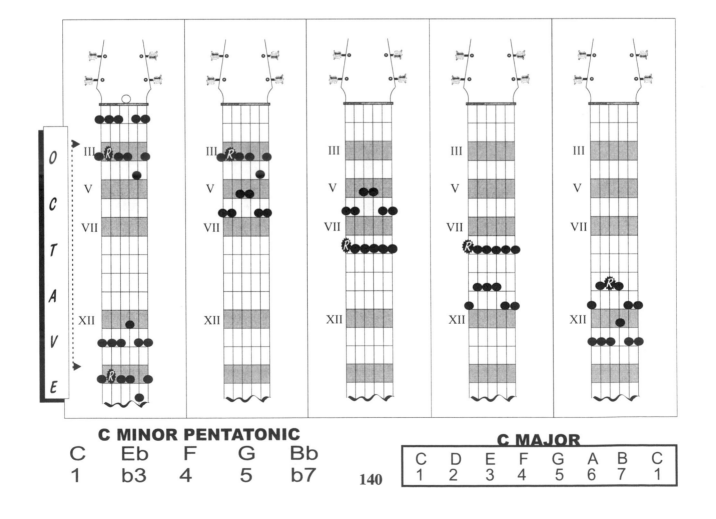

C MINOR PENTATONIC				
C	Eb	F	G	Bb
1	b3	4	5	b7

C MAJOR							
C	D	E	F	G	A	B	C
1	2	3	4	5	6	7	1

C MINOR PENTATONIC SCALE -OPEN POSITION

C MINOR PENTATONIC SCALE -POSITION III

C MINOR PENTATONIC SCALE -POSITION V

C MINOR PENTATONIC SCALE -POSITION VIII

C MINOR PENTATONIC SCALE -POSITION XI

C MINOR PENTATONIC SCALE -POSITION XIII

The 5 basic shapes of a D7 chord.

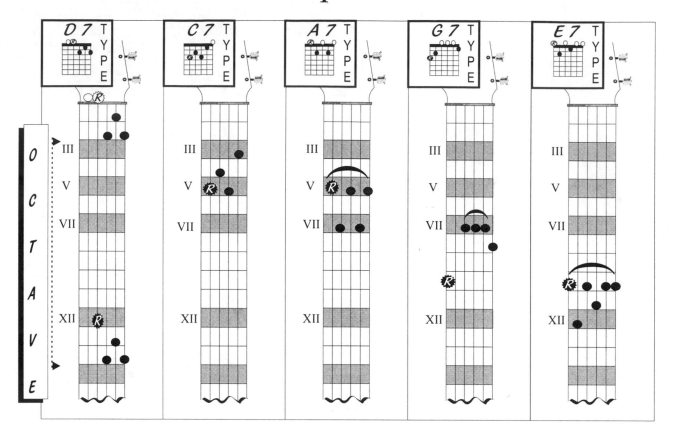

The 5 basic shapes of a D Minor Pentatonic scale.

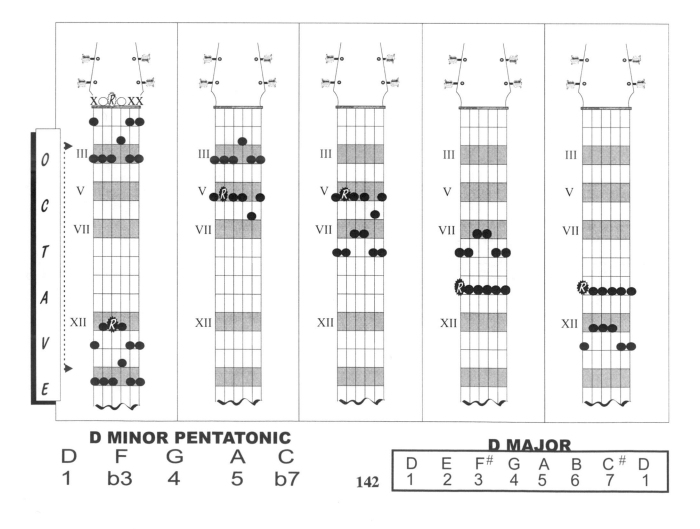

D MINOR PENTATONIC

D	F	G	A	C
1	b3	4	5	b7

D MAJOR

D	E	F#	G	A	B	C#	D
1	2	3	4	5	6	7	1

142

D MINOR PENTATONIC SCALE -OPEN POSITION

D MINOR PENTATONIC SCALE -POSITION III

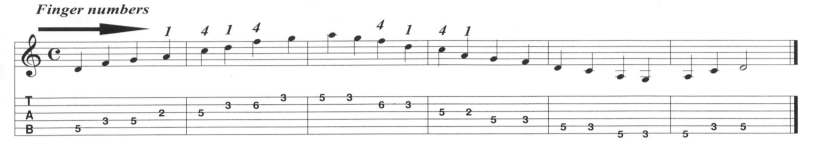

D MINOR PENTATONIC SCALE -POSITION V

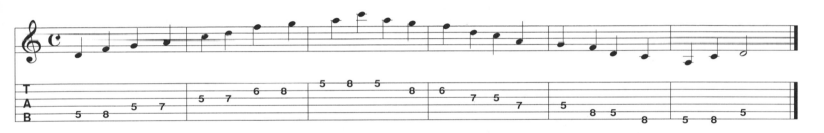

D MINOR PENTATONIC SCALE -POSITION VII

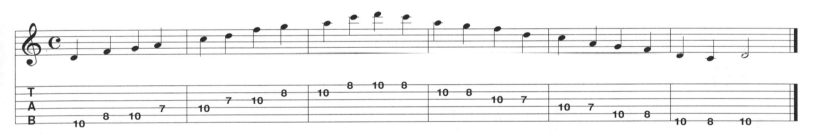

D MINOR PENTATONIC SCALE -POSITION X

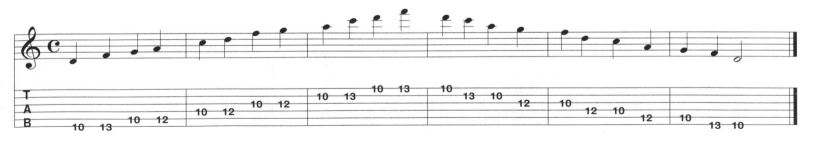

D MINOR PENTATONIC SCALE -POSITION XII

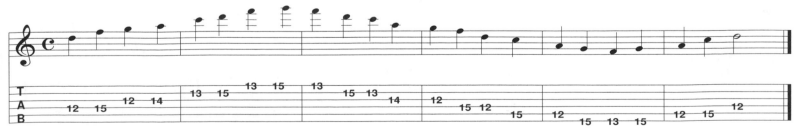

The Linking System: Blues Scales

To learn to play the 5 positions of the E BLUES scale,
center your thinking around 5 dominant chords in the open position:

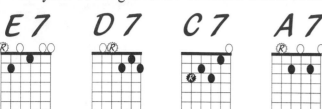

E 7   D 7   C 7   A 7   G 7

BLUES SCALES ARE MINOR
PENTATONIC SCALES WITH
THE ADDITION OF ONE
EXTRA NOTE; THE FLATTED
FIFTH DEGREE OF
THE MAJOR SCALE.   *Flat five*   **b5**

E BLUES -POSITIONS I & XII

LINK

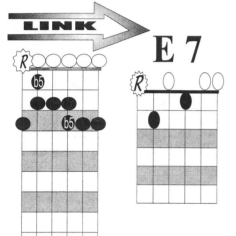

E 7

	1	2	3	4	5	6	7	8/1
E MAJOR:	E	F#	G#	A	B	C#	D#	E

E BLUES:	E		G	A	Bb	B		D	E
	1		b3	4	b5	5		b7	1

E 7 type   Associate this scale, in the open & twelfth position with an E7 type of chord. Of course, an E Blues scale has many more applications than just E7. *(see pages 53 and 68 also.)*   **E7**

E7 CHORD
POSITION II

E BLUES -second position

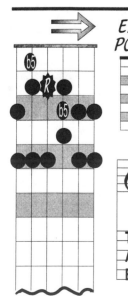

D 7 type   MOVING A D7 CHORD UP THE NECK BY TWO FRETS YEILDS E7   **D7**

144

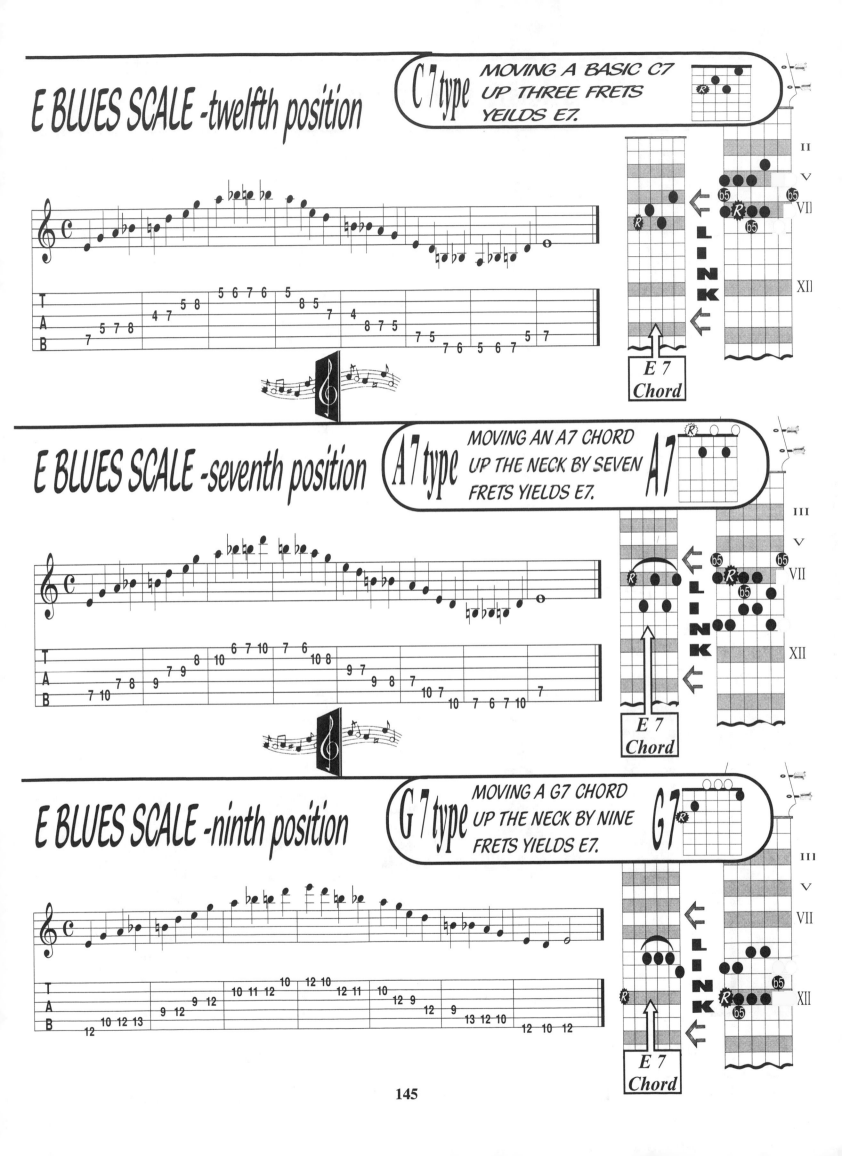

E BLUES SCALE -twelfth position

C7 type — MOVING A BASIC C7 UP THREE FRETS YEILDS E7.

E 7 Chord

E BLUES SCALE -seventh position

A7 type — MOVING AN A7 CHORD UP THE NECK BY SEVEN FRETS YIELDS E7.

E 7 Chord

E BLUES SCALE -ninth position

G7 type — MOVING A G7 CHORD UP THE NECK BY NINE FRETS YIELDS E7.

E 7 Chord

The 5 basic shapes of a D7 chord.

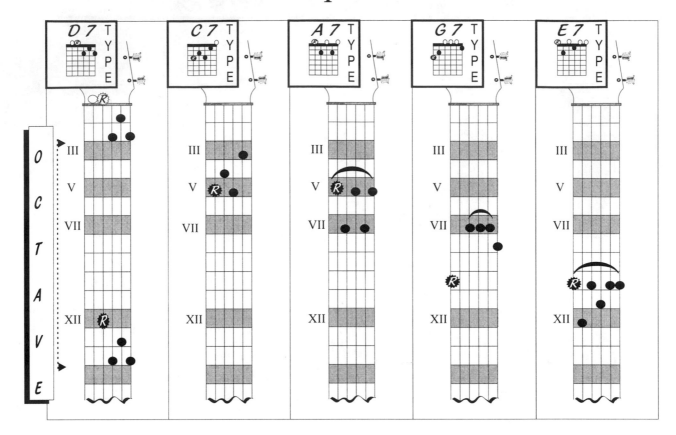

The 5 basic shapes of a D BLUES scale.

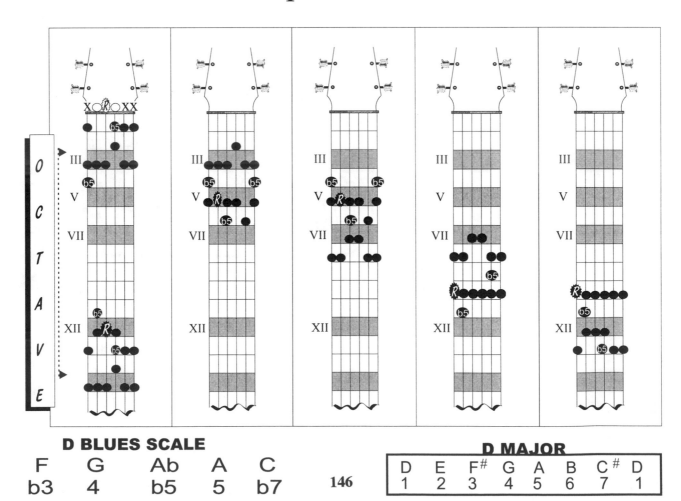

D BLUES SCALE

D	F	G	Ab	A	C
1	b3	4	b5	5	b7

146

D MAJOR

D	E	F#	G	A	B	C#	D
1	2	3	4	5	6	7	1

The 5 basic shapes of a G 7 chord.

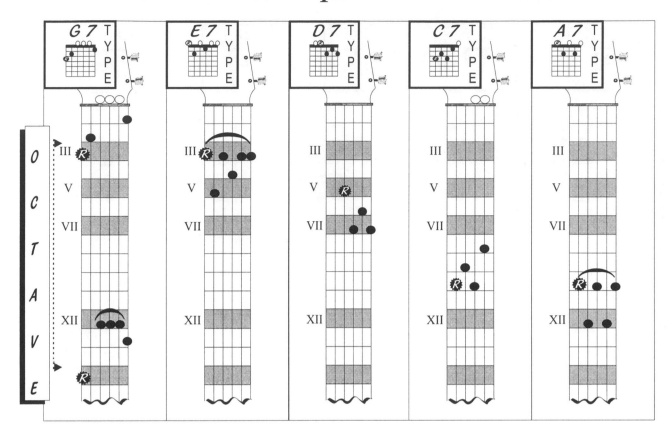

The 5 basic shapes of a G BLUES scale.

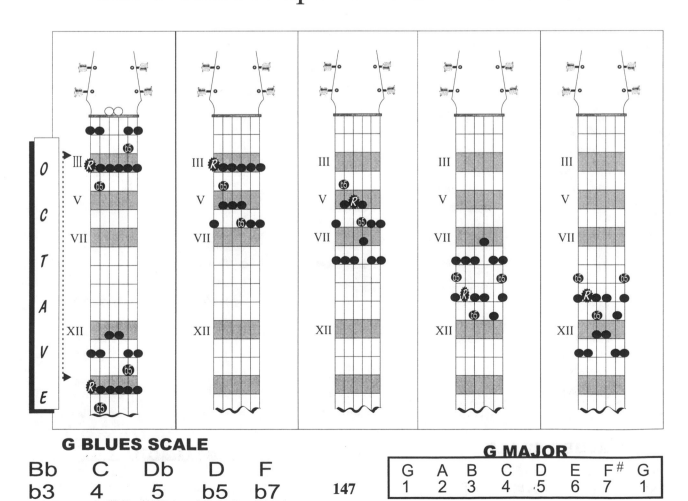

G BLUES SCALE

G	Bb	C	Db	D	F
1	b3	4	5	b5	b7

147

G MAJOR

G	A	B	C	D	E	F#	G
1	2	3	4	5	6	7	1

The 5 basic shapes of an A 7 chord.

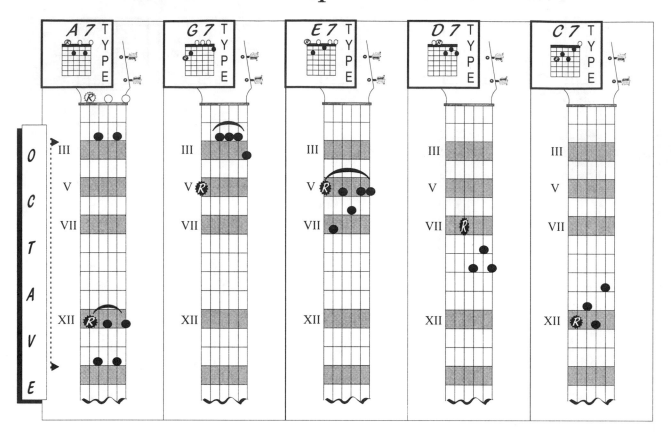

The 5 basic shapes of an A BLUES scale.

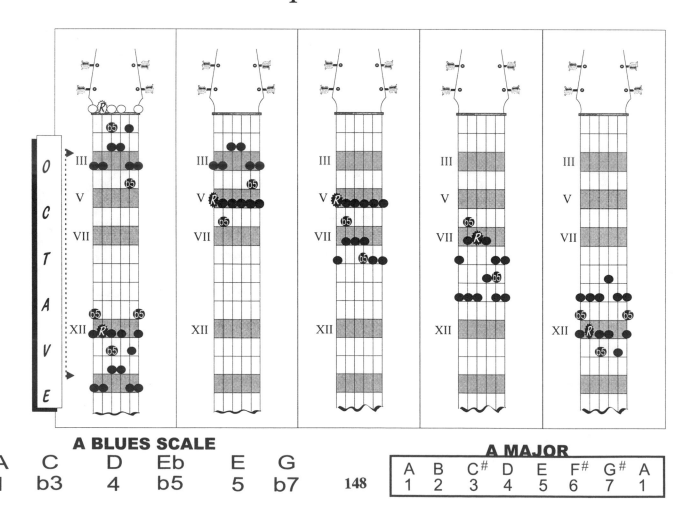

A BLUES SCALE						
A	C	D	Eb	E	G	
1	b3	4	b5	5	b7	

148

A MAJOR							
A	B	C#	D	E	F#	G#	A
1	2	3	4	5	6	7	1

The 5 basic shapes of a C7 chord.

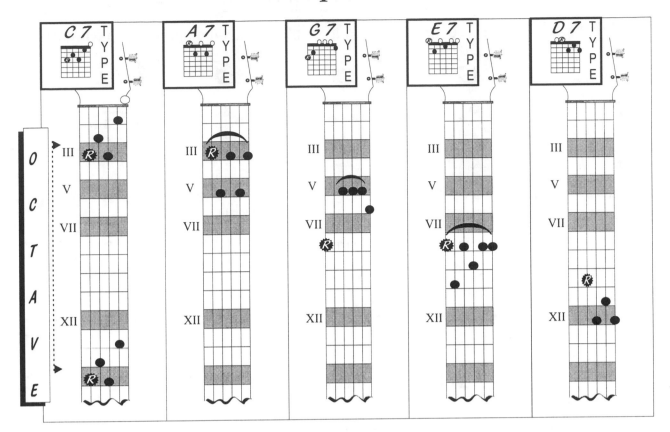

The 5 basic shapes of a C BLUES scale.

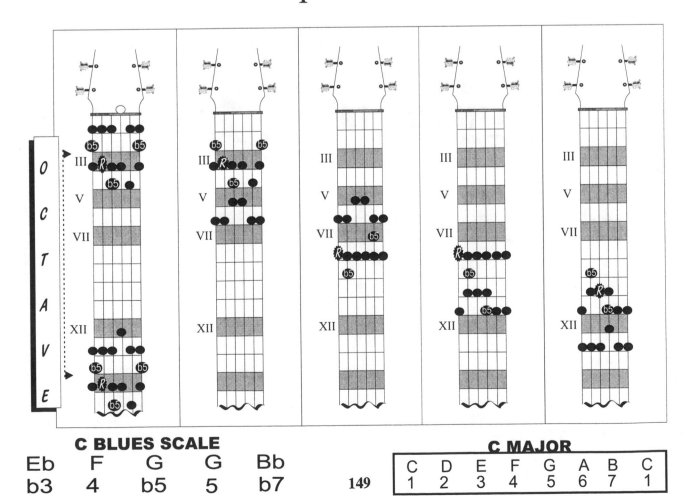

C BLUES SCALE								
C	Eb	F	G	G	Bb			
1	b3	4	b5	5	b7			

149

C MAJOR						
C	D	E	F	G	A	B	C
1	2	3	4	5	6	7	1

The Linking System: Major Pentatonics.

Approach MAJOR PENTATONIC scales as related to 5 interconnected shapes of a Major 6th chord.

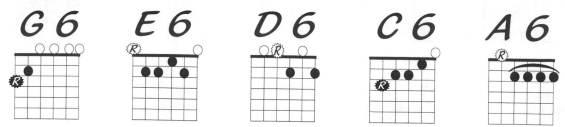

G 6   E 6   D 6   C 6   A 6

Apply the CAGED SYSTEM to 5 open string chords *(G6, E6, D6, C6, A6)* to obtain the **CHORD LINKS** as I have illustrated below. Associating each scale form you learn with a corresponding chord shape makes learning, playing and changing keys much easier.

G MAJOR	1	2	3	4	5	6	7	8/1
	G	A	B	C	D	E	F#	G

	1	2	3		5	6		1
G MAJOR PENTATONIC	G	A	B		D	E		G

G Major pentatonic -open position

G 6 type

Link the G Major pentatonic scale in the open position, with a G6. Of course a **G Major pentatonic** scale has many more musical applications than just G6. *(see pg. 60, 61, 62, 69 & 71)*

LINK WITH

G 6 -Open Position

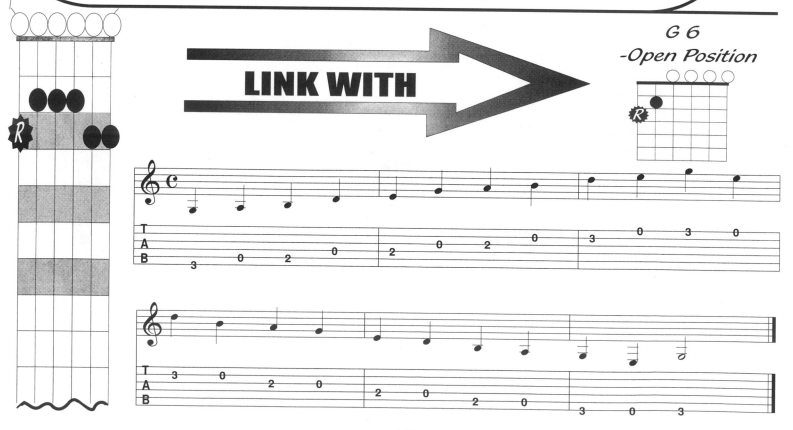

G Major pentatonic -second position

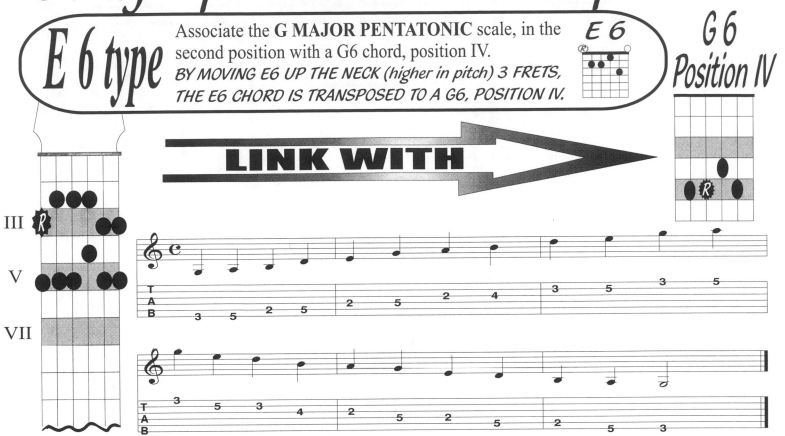

E 6 type Associate the **G MAJOR PENTATONIC** scale, in the second position with a G6 chord, position IV. *BY MOVING E6 UP THE NECK (higher in pitch) 3 FRETS, THE E6 CHORD IS TRANSPOSED TO A G6, POSITION IV.*

E 6

G 6 Position IV

LINK WITH

G Major pentatonic -fifth position

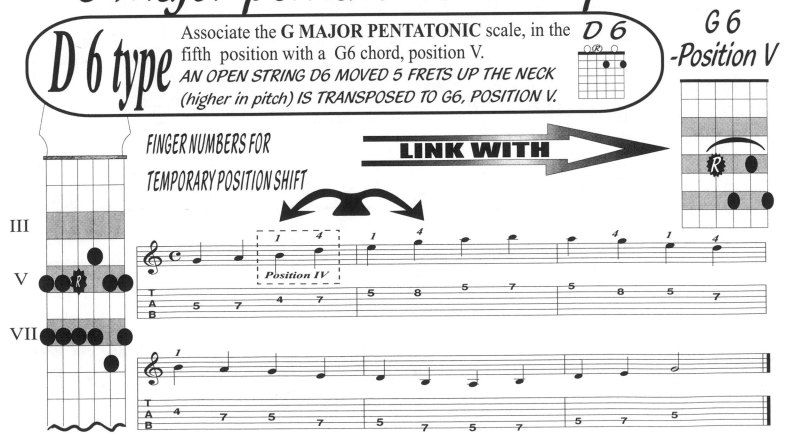

D 6 type Associate the **G MAJOR PENTATONIC** scale, in the fifth position with a G6 chord, position V. *AN OPEN STRING D6 MOVED 5 FRETS UP THE NECK (higher in pitch) IS TRANSPOSED TO G6, POSITION V.*

D 6

G 6 -Position V

LINK WITH

FINGER NUMBERS FOR TEMPORARY POSITION SHIFT

G Major pentatonic -seventh position

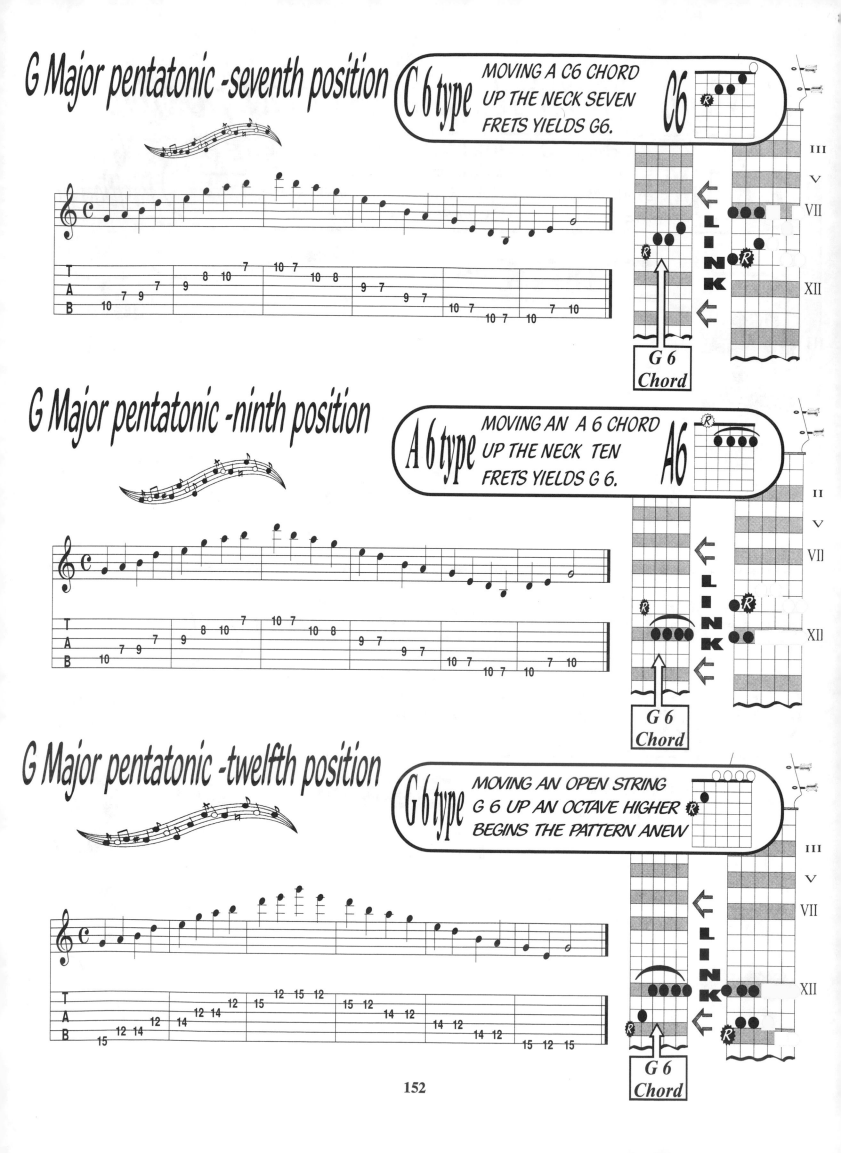

C 6 type — MOVING A C6 CHORD UP THE NECK SEVEN FRETS YIELDS G6.

G Major pentatonic -ninth position

A 6 type — MOVING AN A 6 CHORD UP THE NECK TEN FRETS YIELDS G 6.

G Major pentatonic -twelfth position

G 6 type — MOVING AN OPEN STRING G 6 UP AN OCTAVE HIGHER BEGINS THE PATTERN ANEW

Major Pentatonic Scale Reference Charts

1	2	3	5	6	1	
C	D	E	G	A	C	C MAJOR PENTATONIC
G	A	B	D	E	G	G MAJOR PENTATONIC
D	E	F#	A	B	D	D MAJOR PENTATONIC
A	B	C#	E	F#	A	A MAJOR PENTATONIC
E	F#	G#	B	C#	E	E MAJOR PENTATONIC
B	C#	D#	F#	G#	B	B MAJOR PENTATONIC
F#	G#	A#	C#	D#	F#	F# MAJOR PENTATONIC

THEORY: THE PENTATONIC SCALES

RELATIVES

A minor

A B C D E F G A
1 2 ^{b}3 4 5 ^{b}6 ^{b}7 1

C Major

C D E F G A B C
1 2 3 4 5 6 7 1

RELATIVES

A MINOR PENTATONIC

1 ^{b}3 4 5 ^{b}7
A $^{(\natural)}$C D E $^{(\natural)}$G

C MAJOR PENTATONIC

1 2 3 5 6
C D E G A

RELATIVITY

The note **"C#"** is the normally occurring third in an **A Major scale.** A flatted third in this case is **"C$\natural$"**—a regular **"C"** note.

The same thing holds true for the seventh note of an **A Major scale** which naturally occurs as a **"G#."** The flatted seventh note of an A Major scale is therefore **"G$\natural$"** *(G natural)*.

Just as **C Major** & **A minor** are relative keys, those which share the same notes and key signature. **C Major pentatonic** & **A minor pentatonic** are also relatives. If you know how to play **C Major pentatonic** it also means that you know how to play **A minor pentatonic** because they are exactly the same thing: containing the same notes and employing the same fingering.

G Major pentatonic *(pg. 150)* and **E minor pentatonic** *(pg. 132)* also have this special relationship. For more on this most exciting and useful feature of playing pentatonic scales see pages 162 - 164.

	1	2	3	5	6	1
C MAJOR PENTATONIC	C	D	E	G	A	C
F MAJOR PENTATONIC	F	G	A	C	D	F
Bb MAJOR PENTATONIC	Bb	C	D	F	G	Bb
Eb MAJOR PENTATONIC	Eb	F	G	Bb	C	Eb
Ab MAJOR PENTATONIC	Ab	Bb	C	Eb	F	Ab
Db MAJOR PENTATONIC	Db	Eb	F	Ab	Bb	Db
Gb MAJOR PENTATONIC	Gb	Ab	Bb	Db	Eb	Gb

The 5 basic shapes of an E 6 chord.

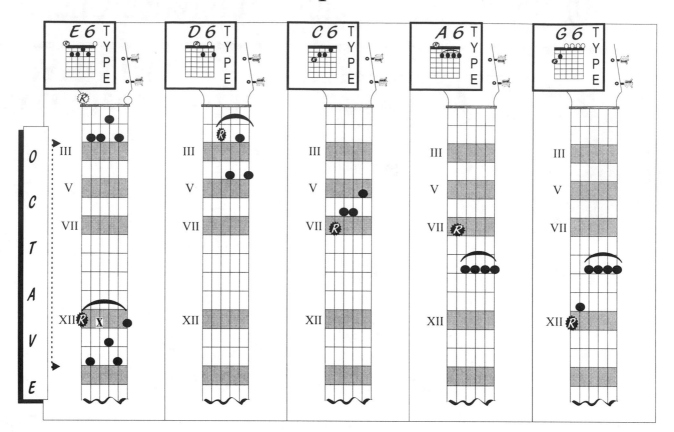

The 5 basic shapes of an E Major Pentatonic scale.

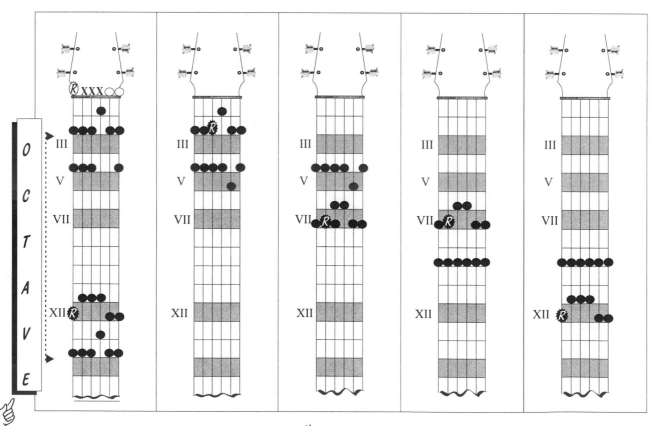

REMEMBER,
 E MAJOR & C# MINOR ARE RELATIVES:
THEY CONTAIN THE EXACT SAME NOTES AND
SHARE A KEY SIGNATURE.

E F# G# B C# E ⟵ E Major Pentatonic

C# minor Pentatonic ⟶ C# E F# G# B C#

E MAJOR PENTATONIC SCALE -OPEN POSITION

E MAJOR PENTATONIC SCALE -POSITION II

E MAJOR PENTATONIC SCALE -POSITION IV

E MAJOR PENTATONIC SCALE -POSITION VI

E MAJOR PENTATONIC SCALE -POSITION IX

E MAJOR PENTATONIC SCALE -POSITION XI

The 5 basic shapes of a D 6 chord.

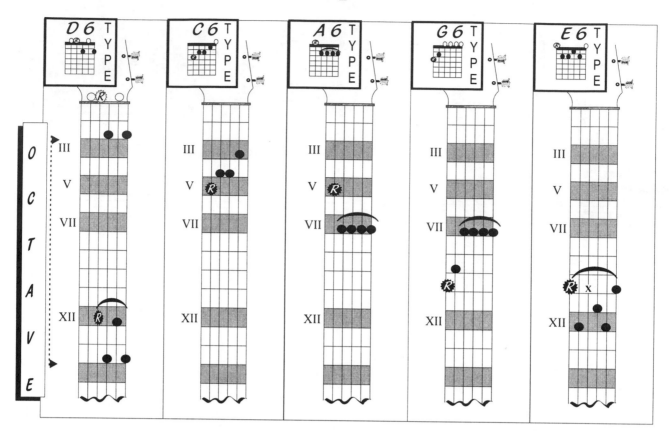

The 5 basic shapes of a D Major Pentatonic scale.

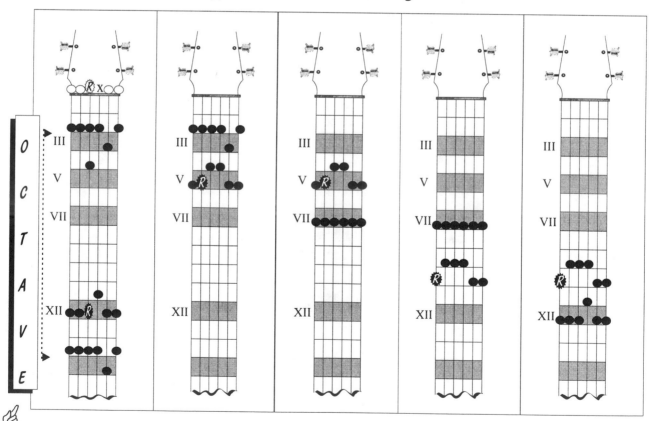

REMEMBER,
   D MAJOR & B MINOR ARE RELATIVES:
THEY CONTAIN THE EXACT SAME NOTES AND
SHARE A KEY SIGNATURE.

D E F♯ A B D ⟵ *D Major Pentatonic*

B minor Pentatonic ⟹ B D E F♯ A B

D MAJOR PENTATONIC SCALE -OPEN POSITION

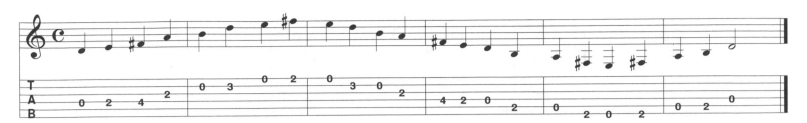

D MAJOR PENTATONIC SCALE -POSITION II

D MAJOR PENTATONIC SCALE -POSITION IV

D MAJOR PENTATONIC SCALE -POSITION VII

D MAJOR PENTATONIC SCALE -POSITION X

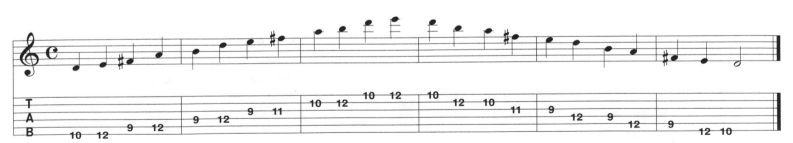

D MAJOR PENTATONIC SCALE -POSITION XII

The 5 basic shapes of a C 6 chord.

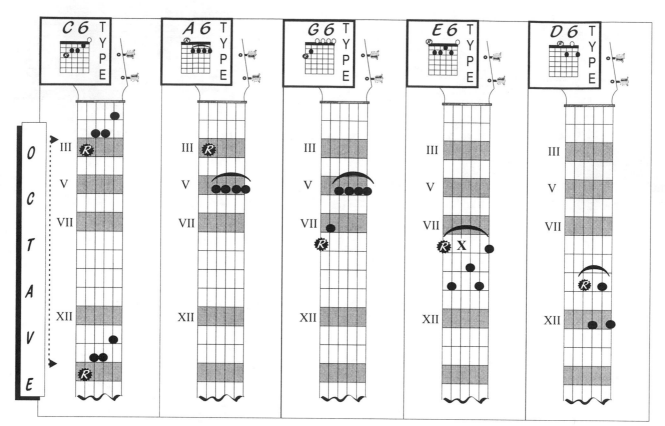

The 5 basic shapes of a C Major Pentatonic scale.

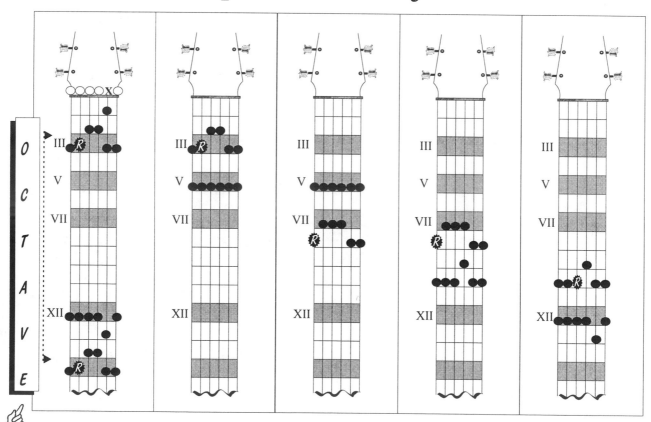

REMEMBER,
C MAJOR & A MINOR ARE RELATIVES:
THEY CONTAIN THE EXACT SAME NOTES AND
SHARE A KEY SIGNATURE.

C D E G A C ⟵ *C Major pentatonic*

A minor pentatonic ⟶ *A C D E G A*

C MAJOR PENTATONIC SCALE -OPEN POSITION

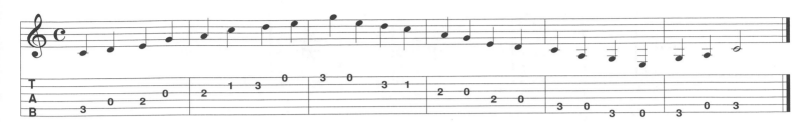

C MAJOR PENTATONIC SCALE -POSITION II

C MAJOR PENTATONIC SCALE -POSITION V

C MAJOR PENTATONIC SCALE -POSITION VII

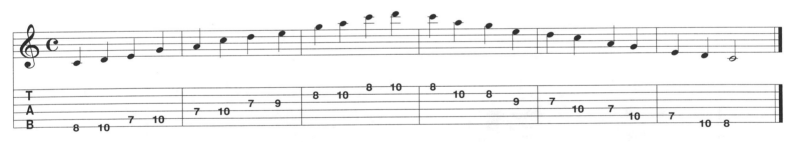

C MAJOR PENTATONIC SCALE -POSITION X

C MAJOR PENTATONIC SCALE -OPEN POSITION

159

The 5 basic shapes of an A 6 chord.

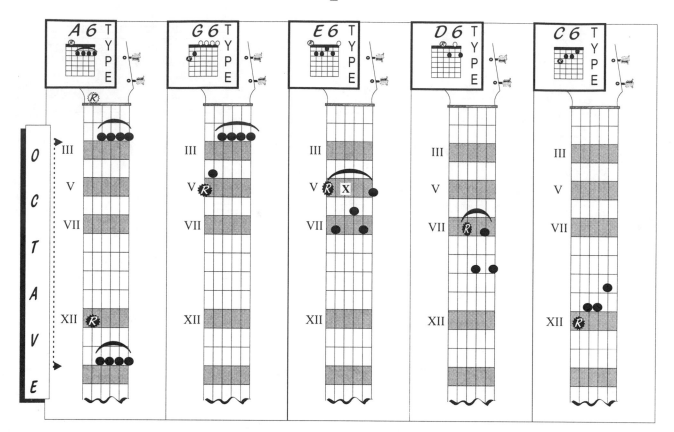

The 5 basic shapes of an A Major Pentatonic scale.

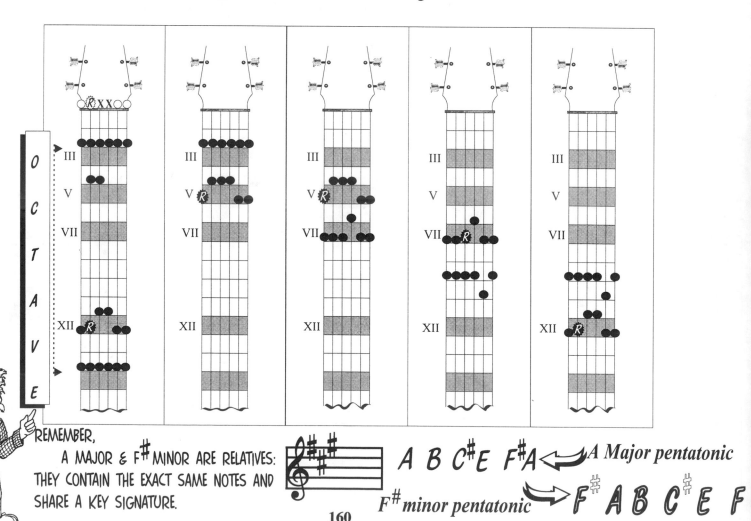

REMEMBER,
A MAJOR & F# MINOR ARE RELATIVES:
THEY CONTAIN THE EXACT SAME NOTES AND
SHARE A KEY SIGNATURE.

A B C# E F#A ← A Major pentatonic

F# minor pentatonic ⇒ F# A B C# E F

A MAJOR PENTATONIC SCALE -OPEN POSITION

A MAJOR PENTATONIC SCALE -POSITION II

A MAJOR PENTATONIC SCALE -POSITION IV

A MAJOR PENTATONIC SCALE -POSITION VII

A MAJOR PENTATONIC SCALE -POSITION IX

A MAJOR PENTATONIC SCALE -POSITION XI

161

PENTATONIC SOLOING CONCEPTS

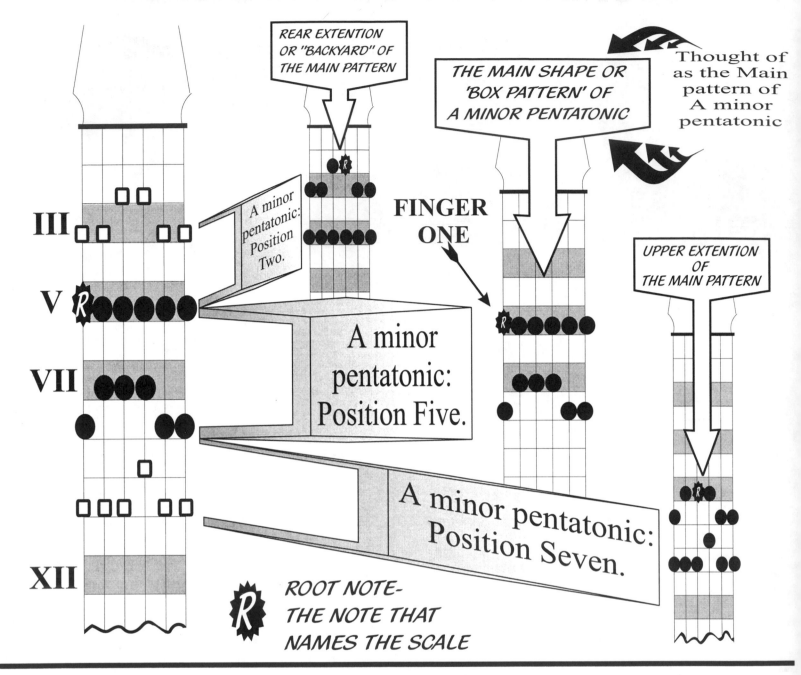

REAR EXTENTION OR "BACKYARD" OF THE MAIN PATTERN

THE MAIN SHAPE OR 'BOX PATTERN' OF A MINOR PENTATONIC

Thought of as the Main pattern of A minor pentatonic

A minor pentatonic: Position Two.

FINGER ONE

A minor pentatonic: Position Five.

UPPER EXTENTION OF THE MAIN PATTERN

A minor pentatonic: Position Seven.

R — ROOT NOTE - THE NOTE THAT NAMES THE SCALE

There are two things which give a scale its sound;

1.) The *formula,* or distances between the notes.

2.) The *chord* or *chord progression* against which the scale is being sounded.

formula: $1\frac{1}{2}$ 1   1 $1\frac{1}{2}$ 1

Spelling: A   C   D   E   G   A

STEP & A HALF   WHOLE STEP   WHOLE STEP   STEP & A HALF   WHOLE STEP

In the case of *A minor pentatonic* a rockin', bluesy or funky sound will result if the song is a **blues progression** in the **Key of A** *(A7, D7 & E7)* or a rock song in the **Key of A** such as Louie Louie *(A, D, Emi)* or Wild Thing *(A, D, E)*. Most three chord rock songs that start with an A chord could be considered in the **Key of A**.

Blues songs in the **Key of A minor** *(Ami, Dmi & Emi)* will also accept an *A minor pentatonic* as will a one chord vamp consisting of an **A, A minor** or **A7 chord**. There can be no argument as to the minor pentatonic scale being the most used sound in pop, rock & blues lead playing.

The important point on this page is that the very well known box pattern is played in reference to a root on string six. On that root note in your first finger.

A MINOR PENTATONIC MAIN BOX PATTERN

TWO SOUNDS, TWO EFFECTS: ONE SCALE.

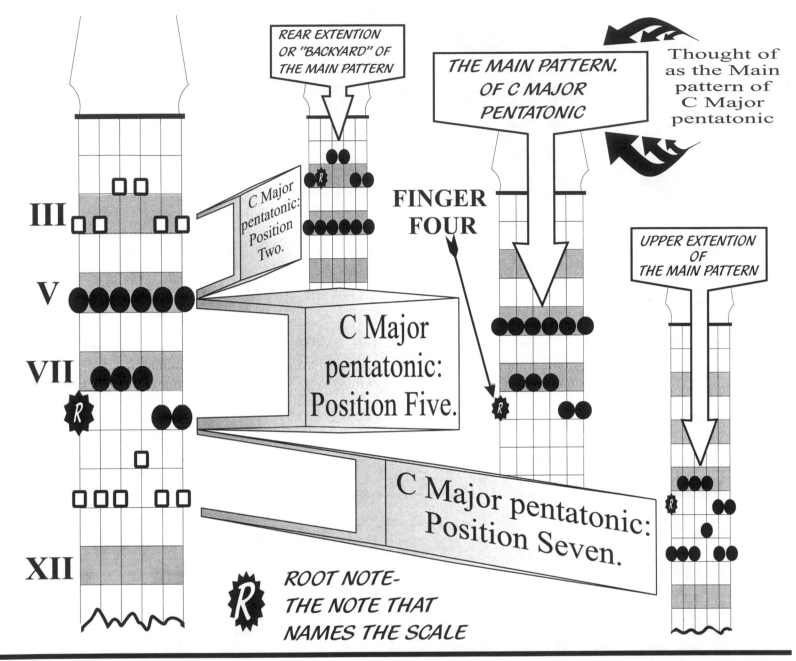

REAR EXTENTION OR "BACKYARD" OF THE MAIN PATTERN

THE MAIN PATTERN. OF C MAJOR PENTATONIC

Thought of as the Main pattern of C Major pentatonic

C Major pentatonic: Position Two.

FINGER FOUR

UPPER EXTENTION OF THE MAIN PATTERN

C Major pentatonic: Position Five.

C Major pentatonic: Position Seven.

R ROOT NOTE- THE NOTE THAT NAMES THE SCALE

III
V
VII
XII

The fingering patterns for *C Major pentatonic* and *A minor pentatonic* are virtually identical: the only difference is in the location of the Root note (**R**). The general overall

formula: 1   1   1½   1   1½

Spelling: C   D   E   G   A   C

WHOLE STEP   WHOLE STEP   STEP & A HALF   WHOLE STEP   STEP & A HALF

musical effect of a lead guitar solo based on a *C Major pentatonic* is sweet melodic and beautifully tuneful provided its sounded against a song or chord progression in the **KEY OF C MAJOR**. Blues songs, love songs, rock ballads, twangy country tunes or jumpin' swing numbers in the **KEY OF C** are all suitable canvases upon which a *C Major pentatonic* scale could be painted. A one chord vamp consisting of a chord in the **C Major family** or **C Dominant family** will accept the nice flowing melodies created by a *C Major pentatonic* scale.

This one scale shape has two names, two sounds and two wonderful, somewhat opposite applications. This is one of the secrets of lead guitar playing.

The important point on this page is that the well known box pattern is played in reference to a root note on string six.

C MAJOR PENTATONIC MAIN BOX PATTERN

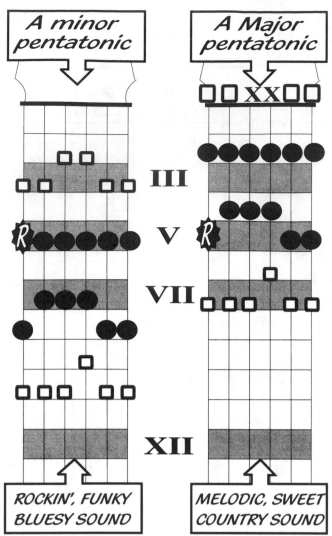

Same Pattern, new location: Two very different sounds.

1.) A minor pentatonic:

When the main box pattern of a pentatonic scale fingering is played in the fifth position, finger one is on the note "A". Look at this as the root note of *A minor pentatonic* and be aware of the rear and upper extensions as I have diagrammed on this and pages 145 & 146.

This scale is reminiscent of Eric Clapton, Buddy Guy, Robby Kreiger of the Doors and Stevie Ray Vaughn to name a few. *A minor pentatonic* will give you a funky, rockin' and bluesy soundin the **KEY OF A**. Definitely the number one scale in pop, rock, blues, soul and funk lead guitar playing.

2.) A Major pentatonic:

When the main box pattern of a pentatonic scale fingering is played in the second position, finger four is on the note "A". Look at this as the root note of *A Major pentatonic* and be aware of the rear and upper extensions as I have diagrammed on this and pages 137, 145 & 146.

The sound of the *Major pentatonic* scale is sort of the opposite of the *minor pentatonic* scale. Use the *Major pentatonic* when you want a sweet, pretty or melodic sound in the **KEY OF A**.

Here's is the really cool part: The fingering patterns are exactly the same only the entire scale shape *(including rear & upper extensions)* is located in a different spot, three frets away.

Same Pattern, new location: Two very different sounds.

1.) C Major pentatonic:

When the main box pattern of a pentatonic scale fingering is played in the fifth position, finger four is on the note "C". Look at this as the root note of *C Major pentatonic* and be aware of the rear and upper extensions as I have diagrammed on this and pages 139, 145 & 146.

The sound of the *Major pentatonic* scale is a sweet, pretty or melodic one. I first learned this as the *"Country Scale"* because it is a general feature of country rock and most Nashville type of styles. The **Allman Bros.**, **Outlaws** and **Marshall Tucker Band** made 70's era hit records using the *Major pentatonic* scale.

2.) C minor pentatonic:

When the main box pattern of a pentatonic scale fingering is played in the eighth position, finger one is on the note "C". Look at this as the root note of *C minor pentatonic* and be aware of the rear and upper extensions as I have diagrammed on this and page 123. Use this scale for a rock, blues or funky sound in the **KEY OF C**.

The scale shapes and fingering patterns *C minor pentatonic* and *C Major pentatonic* are exactly the same only the main box patterns *(including rear & upper extensions)* are located in two different spots, three frets away.

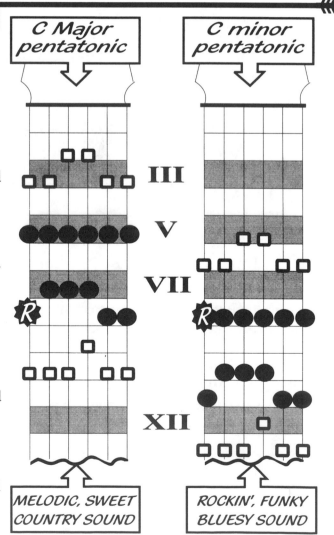

164

This book is intended to be a comprehensive study of the most important scale skills for any guitar student, teacher or player. The material is in a logical, cumulative order beginning with basic information, open string scales and ending with an in depth analysis of position playing techniques in use by top professionals. Use the following guidelines as you design a course of study. Be comfortable with the concepts on each line before progressing to the next. Read this page at least once every month.

BEGINNING.

Reading tab and scale diagrams.	**Playing in position**
Traditional guitar notation.	**C Major in position I**
G, D, A, E, F & Bb Major Pos. I	**Melodies in Position I**
Musical alphabet.	**Flats & sharps.**
Chromatic scale.	**Half step, Whole step, Octave.**
Note names on string six.	**Note names on string five.**

PROGRESSING.

Movable scales.	**Root 6 Major, Root 5 Major.**
Theory of Major Scale.	**Scale Spelling vs. Scale Formula**
Names of notes in all 12 Major scales.	**Circle of fifths.**
Minor pentatonic: Root 6, Root 5.	**Blues scale Root 6, root 5.**
Pure minor: Root 6, Root 5	**Major pentatonic: Root 6, Root 5**

Applications of Major, minor, pentatonic and blues scales.

ADVANCING.

5 position thinking.	**CAGED system.**
LINKING SYSTEM	**5 positions of C Major.**
5 positions of all 12 Major scales.	**Open position C minor.**

A, B, C, D, E, F & G minor scales in the open position

Names of notes in all 12 minor scales.	**Concept of pure minors.**
Sound of pure minor.	**Concept of relative minors.**
Name all 12 relative minors.	**5 positions of all 12 minor scales.**

Write out all 12 key signatures on music paper by memory.

BEGINNING.

5 positions of all 12 minor pentatonic scales.

5 positions of all 12 blues scales.	**Concept of relative pentatonics.**

5 positions of all 12 Major pentatonic scales.

~ Notes ~

~ *Notes* ~

~ *Notes* ~